ZERO POPULATION GROWTH: Implications

Joseph J. Spengler, Editor

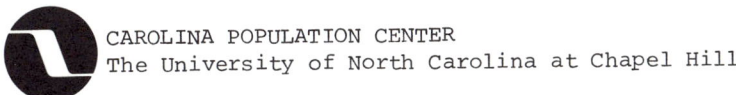

CAROLINA POPULATION CENTER
The University of North Carolina at Chapel Hill

The Carolina Population Center was created
in 1966 to facilitate research, education, and service
devoted to understanding population phenomena
and solving population-related problems.
The Center serves public and private agencies,
businesses, and the public directly,
in North Carolina and the South,
and provides technical assistance
on population matters to more than 20 nations.
CPC is a part of The University of North Carolina
at Chapel Hill.

©1975
Carolina Population Center
The University of North Carolina at Chapel Hill

Contributors

D. Gordon Bennett, Associate Professor of Geography, The University of North Carolina at Greensboro

Harley L. Browning, Professor of Sociology and Director of the Population Research Center, The University of Texas at Austin

V. Jeffrey Evans, Population Economist, Office of Development Planning, Department of Economic and Community Development, State of Maryland, Annapolis

Charles R. Hayes, Lecturer in Geography, The University of North Carolina at Greensboro

Vira R. Kivett, Research Instructor in Child Development and Family Relations, School of Home Economics, The University of North Carolina at Greensboro

Vincent M. LoLordo, Associate Professor of Psychology, Dalhousie University, Halifax, Nova Scotia

William J. Serow, Associate Professor of Economics and Research Director, Population Studies Center, Tayloe Murphy Institute, University of Virginia, Charlottesville

Joseph J. Spengler, James B. Duke Professor of Economics, Emeritus, Duke University, Durham, North Carolina, and Consultant, Carolina Population Center, The University of North Carolina at Chapel Hill

Alan R. Sweezy, Professor of Economics, Caltech Population Program, California Institute of Technology, Pasadena

Boone A. Turchi, Assistant Professor of Economics, The University of North Carolina at Chapel Hill

Charles M. Weiss, Professor of Environmental Biology and Deputy Chairman, Department of Environmental Sciences and Engineering, School of Public Health, The University of North Carolina at Chapel Hill

Contents

Preface   vii

1. Introduction
   Joseph J. Spengler   1

2. The Economics of Stationary and Declining Population: Some Views from the First Half of the Twentieth Century
   William J. Serow   18

3. The Natural History of the Stagnation Thesis
   Alan R. Sweezy   34

4. Higher Education in the Stationary Population: A Comment on North Carolina's System
   V. Jeffrey Evans   44

5. Speculation on Labor Mobility in a Stationary Population
   Harley L. Browning   56

6. Stationary Populations: Pensions and the Social Security System
   Boone A. Turchi   75

7. Governmental Policy Concerning Population Growth and Distribution in the Piedmont Dispersed City
   Charles R. Hayes and D. Gordon Bennett   95

8. Population--Energy Requirements, Environmental Effects
   Charles M. Weiss   106

9. Characteristics and Needs of an Aging Population in a Southern Metropolitan Area
   Vira R. Kivett   123

10. Varied Perspectives on Crowding
    Vincent M. LoLordo   142

CPC Technical Information Service Library
Cataloging in Publication Data

Zero population growth: implications. Edited by Joseph J.
   Spengler. Chapel Hill, N.C., Carolina Population Center.
   University of North Carolina at Chapel Hill, 1975.
       157p. 23 cm.

   1. Stationary population. 2. Economic factors. 3. Education.
4. Labor force. 5. Social welfare. 6. Policy making.
I. Spengler, Joseph John, 1902-
HB851.S64
ISBN 0-89055-113-8

Preface

Probably a few years hence the subject of this volume will rival the oil shortage in concern and difficulty of accommodation, particularly if the forces now pressing the country's population to a zero-growth level should threaten to press it below that level. A study group set up under the auspices of the Carolina Population Center of The University of North Carolina at Chapel Hill examined the implications of the advent of a stationary population in 1973-74. Their inquiries were supplemented by a complementary session of papers presented at the 20 April 1974 meeting of the Population Association of America in New York and by a historical paper presented (see chap. 2) at the annual meeting, 29-31 May 1974, of the History of Economics Society in Chapel Hill.

The papers described are valuable from a policy as well as an analytical point of view. They do not, of course, isolate all the problems that will arise should the country's population cease to grow, nor do they exhaust the policy options that may prove available. They do, however, point out many of the paths along which solutions may be found and thus could set in motion, albeit belatedly, the extensive inquiry called for by the prospect of something like a stationary population--an inquiry not fully developed in the government-sponsored *Population and The American Future* (Washington, D.C.: U.S. Government Printing Office, 1972). In his message (18 July 1969) creating the commission that produced this report, President Nixon rightly observed that "One of the most serious challenges to human destiny in the last third of this century will be the growth of the population." In advanced countries, however, the real challenges will be those associated with zero population growth.

The difficulties associated with something like zero population growth are much less costly, however, than those encountered by developing countries with populations growing 2 to 2.5 percent, or more, a year. These problems, peculiar to the modern world, accompanied the decline in mortality when it was not offset by a decline in the birth rate. Moreover, they are not easily prevented when the population of a high birth rate developing country lacks the motivation to regulate its numbers.

For illustrative purposes, let us consider a developing country whose population is growing between 2 and 2.5 percent per year, and whose overall life expectancy at birth is in the upper fifties. Only between 50 and 53 percent of its population will be of working age, that is, 18 to 64. If the same population were stationary, about 61 percent of the people would be of working age, and the potential productivity per capita would be 15-20 percent higher under otherwise similar conditions. The dependency burden would be 40 to 60 percent higher if the population were growing 2 to 2.5 percent per year, instead of remaining stationary.

Other disadvantages would be present as well. Population growth at a rate of 2 to 2.5 percent absorbs considerable savings, perhaps 10 to 12.5 percent of a country's national income. When a nation's population is stationary, these savings can be invested in improving productivity and the standard of living. Many developing countries are short of land which is most fertile and capable of conversion into high-yield acreage, or they find it difficult, in an oil-short and exchange-short world, to acquire adequate exchange wherewith to buy essential fertilizer. Continuing population growth intensifies the threat of food shortages in many of these countries. Finally, when a population is growing 2 to 2.5 percent a year, there will probably be too little capital available to absorb this growing population into the urban labor force.

In sum, while the advent of zero population growth requires a nation to make a variety of adjustments, these should prove easy in comparison with the problems confronting many of today's high birth rate developing countries. Therefore, while the short-term prospects for zero population growth are limited to the United States and a few other industrialized nations, the forces and policy considerations leading to the achievement of ZPG are well worth broad international study now--by developed and less developed countries.

1

Introduction

JOSEPH J. SPENGLER

Stationary populations are of two sorts: those which temporarily cease to grow because of catastrophic events and those which cease to grow because of human volition and finally assume stable form at the zero-growth level. It is with the latter, or its possibility, that this collection of essays is concerned. While this volume does not deal with the concomitants of declining population growth, some of the findings are pertinent thereto.

Nongrowth of the former type has often temporarily characterized populations which have grown over the long run, mainly before the nineteenth century. Suppose that a population's crude birth rate has been in the neighborhood of 35 per 1,000 inhabitants and its crude death rate in the neighborhood of 33 per 1,000 inhabitants. Then this population would have been growing about 2 per thousand, or one-fifth of 1 percent per year. Should its food supply be adversely affected, or an epidemic (say of influenza) occur, its death rate will rise and its live birth rate will probably fall somewhat--with the result that for a time deaths will equal or exceed births.

Over man's many millennia of very low population growth probably the periodic upsurges of mortality accounted for occasional cessation of his population growth as well as for the occasional decline in his numbers--declines sometimes very great (e.g., the Black Death). Even between 1750 and 1900 natural increase in less developed regions is estimated to have averaged over the whole period only about 0.4 percent per year, if that. (See

U.N. 1973: chaps. 2 and 5; and U.N. 1971:7.)

Our concern here is with the second type of stationary population--the product of fertility control. It could emerge only in the modern world, a world characterized by the capacity to control fertility effectively and hence counterbalance the low mortality common to populations in the developed world. Even so, stopping population growth--the advent of zero population growth --is a slow, nonexplosive process even as are most demographic processes. Even if fertility is high enough only to balance mortality in the long run, 40 or 50 more years may have to pass before births and deaths come into permanent balance. When this balance is achieved, the age composition of the now stationary population will correspond to that of a life table population, subject to the condition that the birth rate equals the death rate with enough births each year to balance the deaths. Thus if life expectancy at birth is 75 years and births annually number one million, the corresponding stationary population will number 75 million and be characterized by a crude birth rate of 13.33 per 1,000 and an equal crude death rate.

In much of our discussion we assume that a population is stationary. It does not follow, however, that this assumption will prove entirely valid. Births tend to fluctuate from year to year for a variety of reasons--varying business conditions, shifting in the age at which women normally marry, changing the manner in which women time their births, and so on. Moreover, should the growth rate sink below zero and be attended by adverse economic effects, cumulative downward pressure might for a time be exercised on fertility and natality.[1] It is quite possible, therefore, that many populations will fluctuate about a central value corresponding to or in the neighborhood of a zero-growth level and hence continue to experience difficulties associated with fluctuation in both births and deaths.

TREND IN NATURAL INCREASE

With some exceptions natality did not decline markedly until the present century. Accordingly, as Serow shows in chapter 2, it was not until in and after the 1920s that a literature of concern began to take shape in a number of Western countries that their populations might be destined to become stationary. This concern probably reflected military and international political considerations in greater measure than economic considerations. Prior to the 1920s this concern was confined to France whose total fertility and long-run natural increase rate often sank below the replacement level, so that pro-natalist measures had increasing but still inadequate support and were not given very effective form until 1939 (see Calot 1974: chaps. 1, 3, 12;

Spengler 1975).

With the discovery in the 1920s, however, that in a number of countries the net reproduction rate had fallen near to or below the replacement level,[2] papers began to appear, as Serow shows, on stationary population (anticipated already by Cannan in 1895), and some countries began to advocate pro-natalist measures, especially Germany and Italy (Glass 1940). Yet, only a few years earlier, fear of impending population pressure had been widely expressed (see Wolfe 1928). While the outbreak of World War II shifted the major concern of low birth rate countries to military undertakings, family allowance and related measures were widely adopted after if not during this war, partly on grounds of distributive equity (U.N. 1967: chap. 6; U.N. 1972).

Here in the United States the crude birth rate resumed its downward trend in the 1920s after an immediate postwar upsurge, continuing to decline until the early 1930s--this at a time when several leading government publications on population trends were still excluding discussion of birth control (see NR 1938; Spengler 1972). Then the crude birth rate began to rise, peaking after the close of the war and remaining near this peak until the late 1950s, only to decline again and by the early 1970s to fall below the early 1930s level. By 1968 the intrinsic rate of natural increase had sunk to 0.6 percent per year, or almost to the low 0.5 percent level of the war years 1940-44. By mid-1974 birth expectations among married women aged 18-24 averaged only 2.17, 24 percent below the average reported in 1967 and no longer enough to replace the population (U.S. Bureau of the Census 1974). Given this rate, the population could become stable at a less than zero rate of natural increase in about 50 years. Our discussions, however, will concentrate on stationary or other stable populations.

AGE STRUCTURE OF A STATIONARY POPULATION

In table 1.1, I contrast the age structure of the U.S. population in 1970 with that which would result if there were no immigration and total fertility dropped immediately (i.e., in 1972) to the replacement level of 2.11--resulting in a stationary population in 2039. This stationary population would number about 15 million less than if fertility moved gradually to the replacement level and the population became stationary in 2062. In each instance, however, most of the destined growth would be attained by 2025. The age structure of the 1970 population is not stable and hence somewhat misleading since it reflects the postwar upsurge of births and the low birth rates of the 1930s and early 1940s. In the last column the changes in age structure are indicated, reflecting the increase in median age from

27.9 to 37.3 years.

Table 1.1. Stationary Population--United States, 1970-2039

Age	Percent of Population		Change Between 1970 and 2039
	1970	Stationary (2039)	
Under 5	8.38	6.78	-1.60
5-14	19.86	13.51	-6.35
15-19	9.44	6.73	-2.71
20-54	43.44	45.56	+2.12
55-59	4.88	5.88	+1.00
60-64	4.22	5.48	+1.26
65-69	3.34	4.91	+1.57
70 and over	6.01	11.13	+5.12
	99.57	99.98	0
Median age	27.9	37.3	-

SOURCE: U.S. Bureau of the Census (1972:20).

A variety of changes is likely to accompany the advent of an age structure such as is depicted in table 1.1--changes to which adjustment will prove difficult if the economy is not kept very flexible. For the present, however, we need only note that based on age structure, *potential* productivity per capita tends to be higher ceteris paribus in this stationary population than in that of 1970 or in a stable population growing, say, 0.5 or more percent per year. Those aged 20-64 or 18-64 constitute a larger fraction of the stationary population than of either the 1970 population or a growing stable population.

Realization of this potential productivity depends on more than the membership of persons of working age in the labor force, since productivity under commercial conditions tends to exceed that under noncommercial domestic conditions. It also depends on the development and maintenance of a worker's productive capacity, a capacity likely to exceed the requirements of most workers' jobs until later in life.

In the individual case this capacity is conditioned by two sets of determinants, *endosomatic* and *exosomatic*. Endosomatic determinants may include human capital in the form of genetic base, knowledge, experience, state of health, work attitudes, sense of responsibility, and other relevant factors inherent in the individual; exosomatic determinants would be nonhuman capital (factors external to the individual), such as technological and organizational improvements, quantity and quality of relevant instrumental capital and supervisory personnel per worker, and other relevant factors. These two sets of determinants are somewhat complementary to one another, at least in the sense that exosomatic determinants are malleable and hence can be accommodated to the needs and idiosyncrasies of some endosomatic determinants.

Both sets of determinants are subject to depletion as well as to augmentation within limits. Aging is a physiologically dissipative force, though subject within limits to countervaillance by refresher education, cumulation of experience, improvement and preservation of health, together with home, work, and related environments. Accordingly, the degree to which we can realize what we have called the superior potential productivity per head of a stationary population turns on the degree to which the dissipative force of aging can be counteracted.

GENERAL UNEMPLOYMENT AND SLOW OR
ZERO OR NEGATIVE POPULATION GROWTH

Awareness of persisting decline in the rate of population growth, together with persisting unemployment, focused attention on the possibility of a connection. That connection was found in the fact that in the past, population growth had absorbed about half the savings supplied when populations were fully employed, together with the supposition that, given little population growth and hence less need for savings, downward adjustment of the interest rate would not prove equal to balancing savings and investment compatibly with full employment. There emerged what was inaccurately labeled a "stagnation theory"--one based on different grounds, however, than analogous Marxian or institutionalist theories. Fundamentally at issue here was the adequacy of the self-adjusting capacity of the existing capitalist economy, together with compensatory measures if required, to accommodate the advent of a population growing slowly or not at all.

Professor Sweezy (chap. 3) examines the natural history of the stagnation theory, its emergence, the degree of its validity, and changes in the economic framework conditioning its empirical grounding. Professor Serow (chap. 2) describes the ideational background of the stagnation theory and the emergence of an "economics" of stationary and declining populations between 1900 and 1950.

PARTICULAR UNEMPLOYMENT AND POPULATION TRENDS

While decline in the population growth rate can affect the employment level through macroeconomic media or channels, thus giving rise to *general* employment, it may also give rise to particular unemployment in subsets of the total economy. Some industries, lines of activity, or occupations are closely linked to some age groups and hence must adjust as the sizes of such age groups change. The demand for teachers at any given level is a case in point, one analyzed in Dr. Evans's essay (chap. 4). (See also Spengler 1941.)

How persistent such *particular* unemployment will be turns in part upon how specifically trained and hence subjectively or objectively immobile is the unemployed person. If he can carry on ten different activities and is willing to do so, it is much easier for him to find employment than if he has only one activity and is not eager to pursue another. Such job specificity also makes difficult the adjustment of the supply of personnel to effective demand for it.

Consider a city with 10,000 pupils of a given level and a student-teacher ratio of 20 to 1--a staff of 500 teachers. Now suppose 10 percent, or 50, of these teachers need to be replaced and hence produced every year. Then a 6 percent increase in pupils will initially necessitate a 60 percent increase in the annually required output of teachers, from 50 to 50 plus 600 ÷ 20 though eventually 53 per year will suffice. Similarly, should the number of pupils decline by 6 percent, only 20 instead of 50 teachers will initially need to be produced to maintain the pupil-teacher ratio though eventually 47 will be required each year. These two examples illustrate the problems confronted by educational administrators when births and eventually school age children increased about 50 percent between 1945 and 1960 and then declined about 20 percent by 1968. At the local community level net migration may greatly accentuate the impact of increase or decrease in the number of births, impacts which are felt initially at the primary school level and later at the secondary school level.

In his study, Dr. Evans (chap. 4) analyzes the significance of the impact of the coming zero rate of population growth on the higher educational system of the State of North Carolina--college enrollment and changes in the need for educational personnel and facilities. Adjustment to decline in these needs will present difficulties until the annual increment in students at each level settles in the neighborhood of zero. For thereafter replacement of personnel and facilities rather than coping with their increase or decrease will constitute the main task of school administrators and of other administrators similarly situated. While national college enrollment will decline slightly in the 1980s, it will rise again in the 1990s and then gradually level off, as will elementary and secondary enrollment.

VERTICAL MOBILITY IN A STATIONARY POPULATION

The advent of a zero rate of population growth will accentuate barriers to both vertical and horizontal mobility in populations characterized by this rate. Horizontal mobility will be touched on later. Here our concern is vertical mobility, Professor Browning's main theme in chapter 5 wherein some of the barriers are described.

Prolonging life expectancy, especially at age of entry into the labor force, slows upward mobility. For example, according to the 1971 life table for white males, 911 of each 1,000 entering the labor force at age 20 will still be around 30 years later at age 50, competing for a number of preferred jobs which have not increased in the same measure, if at all. Given the life table of 1900 only 750 would survive--reducing competition for preferred jobs by perhaps 20 percent. Again, consider two male stationary or life table populations, one based on a life expectancy of 51.83 years and the other on a life expectancy of 73.9 years. In the former, of each 100 males aged 20-64, about 27 percent are aged 50-64, and in the latter, about 32 percent. Such seniority conditions will result in greater competition for top statuses in society.

Reduction in the access of labor force members aged, say 35-60, to preferred posts in the economy--a result of population and individual aging--will result in increased pressure on employers to modify the wage and salary structure and increase the ratio of wages or salaries at perhaps age 35 to that at around age 55--that is, in reducing the average lifetime earnings profile. Younger persons will require monetary offsets to the lessened access to preferred posts, while persons over 50 will experience more intense competition for preferred posts to which seniority may heighten access. As a result the contribution of seniority to income increase over time will be diminished and the upward slope of individual earnings profiles will be increasingly dominated by the forces which augment individual productivity or bargaining power. After a few years most individuals attain their peak productivity under current working conditions and thereafter it is improvement in these conditions that elevates output and income. Thus an assistant professor usually is about as good as he will ever be after being at his work for five or six years.

SOCIAL SECURITY AND PENSIONS

Professor Turchi (chap. 6) shows how the security of older persons may be endangered by the advent of a stationary population. It will be so endangered if the retirement age is reduced, say to age 55, without reducing the age of entry into the labor force enough to offset this reduction and continue adequate provision of security for the aged and retired in the form of social security and pensions. Ultimately, both forms of payment are on a pay-as-you-go basis. Accordingly, the capacity of those in the labor force to provide this payment depends upon their number vis-à-vis the number of recipients of pensions and social security. There is a critical ratio of recipients to providers. If this ratio is exceeded, providers will resist further increase in the burden of social security and pension benefits and the burden of inflation--should the government seek to supplement social security and pension payments through deficit finance--will be intensified.

Professor Serow indicates that despite increase in potential productivity in a stationary population, coupled with reduction of the relative number of young dependents, continuing increase in (1) the recipient to producer ratio and (2) the ratio of the aggregate bill for social security and pensions to the income flowing to the labor force, will prompt growing resistance to these payments. There is already indirect evidence of this. Because of inflation and erosion of the value of retirement benefits, resistance to retiring early or even at age 65 is increasing. As a result the advancement of younger persons is being slowed down since upper level posts are not being vacated through withdrawal of older occupants.

HORIZONTAL MOBILITY

If, when a population is stationary, the labor force also is stationary, we may label as r the rate at which members of the labor force (L) are removed from it by death, disability, and withdrawal, only to have their places filled by individuals entering the labor force for the first time. Under these conditions maintenance of interoccupational and interindustrial balance depends mainly upon $r L$ which may be called *unattached mobile reserve* since most of its members have not yet become attached physically or subjectively to any particular line of activity. In a population and labor force growing at rate i, this reserve would approximate $(r + i) L$. Accordingly, given ceteris paribus, since $(r + i) > r$, it should be easier to maintain interoccupational balance in a growing than in a stationary population.

Two other conditional reserves exist. The first may be called a *detached potential reserve*. It consists of workers displaced by machinery and improved organization, especially in industries with inelastic demand for products. The second consists of *potential mobiles*, individuals given to job changing and experimentation and responsive to the lure of higher wages. Members of both groups may be on or near the *margin of transference*, ready to move to where other or better paying employment is to be had, unless made at least temporarily disinclined to do so by unemployment benefits or trade-union policy. Drawing upon these two groups, especially the latter, for workers to man expanding activities tends to push up wage levels. Accordingly, when the unattached mobile reserve consists of both $i L$ and $r L$ and hence something like a sufficiency of workers is available to man expanding activities, there will be less upward pressure against wage levels--pressure likely to be conducive to cost-push inflation.

An economy will be more flexible and better able to reduce the costs of mobility if labor is less specific in ability and quite subject to transformation that makes job change easy. This is even more true when capital equipment as well as other job components are transformable and hence facilitative of job change. Under these conditions a great deal of horizontal shifting of the labor force, together with complements to the labor force, is possible. As a result the labor market is less Balkanized and less congenial to wage-increasing efforts in one sector of the market while unemployment prevails in another.

When, on the contrary, labor is highly specialized, unemployment of one specialized category of labor tends to halt its production and empty the pipeline of its supply. Subsequent shortages of this labor category results in wage increases abnormally great in the long run. Such a cobweb-like movement of the supply of specialized labor, somewhat comparable to birth fluctuations, will be more pronounced, of course, in respect to specialists requiring four or five years to produce than to those producible in a year or two. Improved forecasting of longer-run requirements will, however, reduce the constraint imposed on the production of specialized labor by a decline in the short-run demand for its services.

In sum, while preservation of interoccupational balance will encounter more obstacles in a stationary than in a growing population, careful planning can reduce these obstacles.

INNOVATION; CAPITAL FORMATION, INCOME DISTRIBUTION

Output-increasing capital formation per capita should prove higher in a stationary than in a growing population under similar conditions since gross savings will be absorbed by population replacement but not by population growth. Several concomitants of a stationary population will, however, reduce the fraction of the national income that is saved. First, taxes may absorb relatively more of potential savings. Second, given only unitary substitutability of capital for labor and hence constancy in capital's share of income, the return to capital inputs will fall; this may affect adversely both the relative capacity and the disposition of capital-owners to form capital. This decline, moreover, is unlikely to be offset by saving on the part of labor out of its increasing income since savings out of wages and salaries, as distinguished from "profits," tend to be predominantly "rainy-day" in character.

Third, profit prospects may be affected, some believe, by supposedly adverse consequences of aging and by a worsening of expectations that reduces inducements to invest, especially in science, innovation, and new activities.

1. It is argued that just as in a larger population there should be a higher number of potential inventors and innovators so in a growing as compared with a stationary population of given size there should be somewhat more persons of an age with which inventive capacity is highly correlated.

2. If younger persons are better trained than older persons and more favorable to change, then a growing population will enjoy an advantage on both scores inasmuch as it contains relatively more young people.

3. In a stationary population, with its relatively large number of older members, too much decision-making power tends to pass into the hands of older persons with a short time-horizon and conduce to gerontocratic rule.

While statement 2 may possess some validity, statement 1 is not very plausible in a world characterized by free flow of information. The tendency described in statement 3 can be avoided by requiring that a fraction of governing bodies, say at least one-third, be under 50 and another third under 60. It is possible, however, that expectation of continuing population growth as well as of average income growth will be favorable to investment, though this could be partly offset if relatively more persons in a stationary population were financially able to undertake risky ventures.

STATIONARY NUMBER OF BIRTHS

A stationary population is free of an important source of economic and social instability, namely, marked fluctuation in the annual number of births. This phenomenon has been conspicuous over the past 45 years, a period marked by great depression, war, immediate postwar adjustment, and the period succeeding. As suggested above, such fluctuation produces great fluctuation in the demand for population-oriented products, durable goods, and products complementary to these two categories. Upsurges and downsurges move through the economy much as does a large object of prey through the body of a python.

Population upsurges destroy public tranquility under modern conditions. Since crime rates are much higher among younger persons, population upsurges give rise to crime upsurges, which a society is not initially and easily prepared to control. This tendency will be accentuated also if the upsurge in the number of persons entering the labor force results in an unemployment upsurge and a possible swelling of the ranks of those not yet effectively absorbed into society.

POPULATION QUALITY

A stationary population is likely to be characterized by a greater measure of unfavorable genetic and social selection than is a growing population. Even today a relatively large fraction of births is produced by a relatively small fraction of the women of childbearing age. Should the *decline* in births responsible for the advent of a stationary population be concentrated among those of favorable genetic composition and those capable and willing to provide favorable family and local environments to children, the fraction of a nation's births produced under very favorable conditions will diminish. The relative number of births produced under unfavorable conditions will increase. As a result the population will in time prove less capable of coping with the problems confronting it.

POPULATION DISTRIBUTION AND THE AGED

With the development of individualized transport and decline in the ratio of the cost of using such transport to the incomes of users, population mobility and habitat dispersal increased.

Accordingly, while population concentration over the United States terrain as a whole remains great, there has been deconcentration or absence of concentration in local subregions.

Roughly illustrative is the Piedmont Dispersed City, described by Professors Charles R. Hayes and D. Gordon Bennett in chapter 7. This is not a city in the usual meaning, but a number of functionally interrelated small cities and towns constituting a kind of metropolitan subregion. As a result relatively low densities characterize most of the population centers within the dispersed city. Accordingly, a variety of options remain as to how population should be distributed over this dispersed city, but there is neither a set policy nor adequate provision for reflecting the wants of the underlying population.

Reconciliation of the options discussed by Hayes and Bennett is complicated by the business of meeting the varied needs of the aged, among them transportation (see Falcocchio and Cantilli 1974; Bennett and Kivett 1974), which Dr. Kivett discusses in chapter 9. Her careful study of the needs of an aging population in a Southern metropolitan area points up both deficiencies in the means currently available for satisfying these needs and how currently unmet needs may be better served. Moreover, while her study deals with a concrete area, much of what she has found applies to other areas. Her study reveals how these needs vary with income, social status, health, religious attitude, and so on, and how essential information is to developing policies to meet the concrete needs of specific areas.

While the circumstances surrounding older people in the area Dr. Kivett studied are superior to what one encounters in many parts of the United States, they nonetheless are unsatisfactory in many respects and inflation has greatly accentuated these deficiencies. Among rural people some deficiencies are even greater.

In view of the great and rapidly growing number of persons in and over the late 60s and dependent on small social security and pension incomes--now being eroded by inflation--Dr. Kivett's findings are of import far beyond the area she has analyzed both as a source of information and as an indicator of desired social policy. Her study, jointly with that of Hayes and Bennett, points to local problems destined to be accentuated by the rising cost of energy discussed in chapter 8.

MAN-LAND RATIO

Until later in the nineteenth century population pressure was commonly expressed in terms of the ratio of numbers of men to land, sometimes with allowance for differences in the quality or situation of the land. In the course of the nineteenth century, however, many components of man's environment acquired importance until today we think in terms of man's pressure upon the biosphere, or at least upon that part of the biosphere pertinent to man's welfare--the "homosphere," as K. E. Boulding has called it--a part that continues to grow.

While the incidence of this pressure is always local, its origin is both local and external. For with the multiplication and diversification of man's tastes and effective demands, his budget of wants transcends his capacity to satisfy them locally and hence presses him to produce that in which he has a comparative advantage and exchange it for that which he cannot produce economically. Moreover, the limits to this exchange move outward as transport improves and its relative cost declines.

One implication of the growth of exchange in volume, together with a facilitative world price and trade system, is that while the advent of a stationary population can slow the growth of pressure within a country upon its environment, it cannot wholly check this growth. For a country must produce products to pay for imports from abroad, and such production will increase pressure on elements in the local environment--on local ecosystems, land, mineral sources, and so on. This pressure can be counterbalanced in only a small measure by importing pressure-generating products from abroad, since these must be paid for with other products, many of which produce domestic pressure. Thus imports of raw materials increase pressure on the agricultural base, together with ecosystems related to it, in effect changing the points of incidence and perhaps the amount of pressure but not eliminating it.

Increase in man's pressure on his environment or biosphere depends mainly on the growth of his numbers and average income and how his population is distributed in space. The advent of a stationary population is favorable, therefore, in that population growth no longer adds to population pressure and that it may now be easier to improve the distribution of population in space. Moreover, while increase in man's average income as a result of nongrowth of population will increase man's *average* pressure on the biosphere under given conditions, this increase in average income may also facilitate both improvement in a population's distribution and in the development and support of anti-pollution and environment-improving measures.

In chapter 8 Professor Weiss describes the triangle interrelating population, energy, and environment and means of easing problems issuing out of these interrelations. These problems have been intensified in the course of the past two years by the rising cost of energy sources, especially oil, coal, and gas, and by the impact of the great increase in oil prices on the cost of fertilizer and other critical products into whose production petroleum products enter. Moreover, as noted earlier, the need to augment exports, especially of farm products, together with the export-augmenting impact of devaluation of the dollar, has accentuated the forces making for unprecedented increases in the monetary cost of living in the United States.

Unfortunately, slackening of population growth has done virtually nothing to correct this situation. For, as noted earlier, population will not actually cease to grow for a number of decades, and even when it does, pressure will continue to grow but not as rapidly as it would were numbers to continue to grow.

The rising cost of energy will modify the set of circumstances governing population location, population distribution within urban and metropolitan areas, and the character of residential and other construction. For since the price of energy will continue to be relatively high in the future, structures which consume--indeed waste--considerable energy will prove to be too expensive and therefore will be priced out of the market. Fuel shortage may cause individual houses, both suburban or the Levittown-type, to give place to high density clusters which foster land and other economies. Compact cities, such as Dantzig and Saaly (1973) describe, will come into their own, and "spread cities" and urban sprawl will be handicapped by rising costs. At the same time fuel shortage will discourage construction of very large cocoon-like buildings which shut out the outdoors and sometimes encourage daytime population congestion. Fuel economy will also affect the location of economic activities, particularly those which require relatively large amounts of energy, and these in turn will affect the character of transport and the location of population. These changes may prove favorable to the older population since the new transport facilities will be better suited to their needs.

Concentration of dwellings in space may of course increase the flow of pollutants unless adequate countervailing measures are adopted. Accordingly, while compact settlement may make for economy of transport, it may entail somewhat offsetting costs. With increase in average income the costs either of transport and energy, or of pollution control can be borne. But the needs of the aged along these lines may be considered too costly to meet in the absence of compactness of settlement.

EXTREME DENSITY

While extreme population density can coexist temporarily with zero population growth, it is not likely to persist. For, as

Dr. LoLordo shows (chap. 10), although one cannot infer from the behavior of animals living under extreme density just how extreme density affects humans, some independent studies of human behavior indicate a degree of parallelism. Density beyond a certain level may affect man's health adversely and elevate indices of social pathology. To produce these effects density must be highly localized (that is, density per room, rather than per acre).

CONCLUSION

Some problems are not particularly affected by the changes in age structure associated with the rate of population growth. Others vary considerably with age changes. While an upsurge of births and subsequently of teenagers and young adults may temporarily generate serious problems (crime, crowding of institutional facilities, unemployment, intergenerational conflict), demographic changes as a rule are of slow tempo and hence only gradually modify both the structure of a population and its pressure on facilities and resources. Accordingly, it should prove easy for societies to adjust to slow, zero, or slightly negative rates of population growth. Ease of adjustment, however, requires that an economy remain flexible, that man-made barriers not be put in the way of necessary adjustments, and that essential changes (financial, occupational, fiscal) be anticipated in sufficient measure. Unfortunately, the adjustability of an economy to domestic demographic changes may be somewhat restricted by its external commercial and military relations, especially the latter (see Martin 1973), which therefore must be taken into account in national policy formation.

NOTES

1. See, however, T. W. Swan's critique (1962:423-24). Here Swan shows that "the mere fact of 'mutual causation' between two variables is not sufficient to guarantee an unstable equilibrium." One may therefore reason a fortiori that although declining population worsens the socioeconomic environment which in turn depresses fertility, interaction will continue only if the two variables remain sufficiently sensitive to one another. See also Sorokin (1941: chap. 14).

2. R. R. Kuczynski (1928, 1931) was mainly responsible for the currency given this discovery (see especially vol. 1).

REFERENCES

Bennett, D. Gordon; Kivett, Vira R.; and Associates (1974) "Characteristics and Needs of the Population Living Near the Greensboro Business District." Technical Report 12, School of Home Economics. Greensboro: The University of North Carolina at Greensboro.

Calot, Gérard, ed. (1974) "La population de la France." *Population* 29 (special number, June).

Cannan, Edwin (1895) "The Probability of a Cessation of the Growth of Population in England and Wales During the Next Century." *Economic Journal* 5:505-15.

Dantzig, George Bernard and Saaly, Thomas L. (1973) *Compact City*. San Francisco: W. H. Freeman.

Falococchio, J. C. and Cantilli, E. J. (1974) *Transportation and the Disadvantaged*. Lexington, Mass.: Lexington Books.

Glass, David V. (1940) *Population Policies and Movements in Europe*. Oxford: Clarendon.

Kuczynski, Robert René (1928) *Western and Northern Europe*. The Balance of Births and Deaths, vol. 1. Institute of Economics of the Brookings Institution. Publication no. 29, 43. New York: Macmillan.

──────── (1931) *Eastern and Southern Europe*. The Balance of Births and Deaths, vol. 2. Washington: Brookings Institution.

Martin, Laurence (1973) *Arms and Strategy: The World Power Structure Today*. New York: David McKay.

NR (1938) "Censoring a Scientist." *New Republic* (17 August):30-31.

Sorokin, Pitirim A. (1941) *Social and Cultural Dynamics*. Vol. 4. New York: American Book Co.

Spengler, Joseph J. (1941) "Population Trends and the Future Demand for Teachers." *Social Forces* 19:465-76.

──────── (1972) "Numbers Versus Welfare." *Social Science Quarterly* 53:452-58.

──────── (1975) *France Faces Depopulation*. 2d ed. Durham, N.C.: Duke University Press.

Swan, T. W. (1962) "Circular Causation." *Economic Record* 38: 421-28.

United Nations. (1967) *Incomes in a Postwar Europe: A Study of Policies, Growth and Distribution*. Geneva: United Nations.

_____ (1971) *The World Population Situation in 1970*. Population Studies no. 49. ST/SOA/Ser.A/49. New York: United Nations.

_____ (1972) *Measures, Policies and Programmes Affecting Fertility with Particular Reference to National Family Planning Programmes*. New York: United Nations.

_____ (1973) *The Determinants and Consequences of Population Trends*. Vol. 1. Population Studies no. 50. ST/SOA/Ser.A/50. New York: United Nations.

U.S. Bureau of the Census (1972) *Current Population Reports: Illustrative Population Projections for the United States: The Demographic Effects of Alternate Paths to Zero Growth*. Ser. P-25, no. 480. Washington: U.S. Government Printing Office.

_____ (1974) *Current Population Reports: Prospects for American Fertility: June 1974*. Ser. P-20, no. 269. Washington: U.S. Government Printing Office.

Wolfe, A. B. (1928-20) "The Population Problem Since the World War: A Survey of Literature and Research." *Journal of Political Economy* 36:529-59, 662-85; 37:87-120.

2

The Economics of Stationary and Declining Populations: Some Views from the First Half of the Twentieth Century

WILLIAM J. SEROW

THE ECONOMICS OF STATIONARY AND DECLINING POPULATIONS

The sharp decline in fertility experienced in Europe and areas of European settlement during the 1920s and 1930s produced a substantial volume of literature dealing with the possibility of a stationary or declining population and some of the economic problems that would likely be experienced in the event of eventual immobility. Although this was by no means the first interest shown in such a possibility (Spengler[1] suggests that Moheau's 1778 work, *Recherches et considerations sur la population de la France,* pointed to an ultimate decline in France's population), no widespread interest in this problem had existed previously. Some of this concern, however, was foreshadowed by Cannan in 1895, who expected the rate of population increase in England to decline and eventually reach zero (see Wolfe 1928 and Cannan 1895).

Writing in 1929, Lionel Robbins took note of Bowley's (1924) assertion that, with the existing death rate and no increase in births, the population of Great Britain would become stationary sometime during the 1940s (see also Neisser 1944). Although this assertion and others like it did not prove correct--nor was it demographically probable for stationarity to occur so quickly--Robbins did use this context to demonstrate that a stationary population did not necessarily imply a stationary economy. Briefly, Robbins noted the following:

1. The rate of increase of production should diminish unless technological change occurred at a rate higher than then observed.

2. The population would become older and, in general, less adaptable. Consequently, the labor force would be less flexible and the distribution of labor among occupations would be less than optimal.

3. The growth rate of aggregate savings would decline, though little can be said for per capita savings.

4. The composition of consumption would change--"fewer toys, more footwarmers."

5. The demand for goods readily satiable (such as basic foodstuffs) would stabilize.

6. The demand for money would continue to grow, although at an abated rate, since aggregate demand is due in some measure to population size. This effect, notes Robbins, may be partially offset by increasing wealth.

A similar argument is advanced by Hans Staudinger (1936). Staudinger feels that for the old industrial world (Western Europe) technical progress is a dominant force, which can create new demand even with a stationary population. Demand is held to be the major economic force. Interestingly enough, Staudinger feels that for a static economy lacking technology (he suggests India), the Malthusian law is valid and that there is a "vicious" interdependence between population and subsistence.

Much of the concern was triggered by Kuczynski's (1928,1931) analysis of recently observed trends in vital rates, with no attempt made at treating their social cause or economic consequences. Without making explicit forecasts of the future, Kuczynski noted that the fertility observed in some nations as of 1931 (such as Austria, Estonia, and Latvia) was so low that in the absence of a marked increase, these populations would eventually die out, even allowing for most reasonable expectations of reduced mortality. Kuczynski also noted that Russia was then the only European nation with a population growth rate in excess of 1 percent per annum. Several years later, Kuczynski (1938 cited in Weiner 1971:570) also noted the worldwide decline in numbers of whites relative to other races and that the rise of colonialism could be partially explained by demographic factors.[2]

The response to such speculation was widespread. Keynes (1937) noted that the demand for capital, apart from technological changes, increased more or less in proportion to population. Business expectation tended to be based on readily visible present events rather than on prospective changes which might influence the pattern of aggregate demand; and an era of increasing population tends to promote optimism, since estimates of demand for goods and services are more likely to be short of consumers' wishes rather than in excess of them. Consequently, under such conditions, a mistake in judgment leading to a temporary oversupply of capital is more easily rectified. Keynes (1937:13) adds that in the advent of a stationary population:

> . . . we shall . . . be absolutely dependent for the maintenance of prosperity and civil peace on policies of increasing consumption by a more equal distribution of income and of forcing down the rate of interest to make more profitable a substantial change in the length of the period of production. (See Lafitte's 1940 rejoinder.)

Also considering the United Kingdom, Reddaway (1939) attempted to evaluate the probable outlook for the economy. Making the assumption of a continuation of the then existing socioeconomic structure, the absence of a major war (a remarkable assumption considering the 1939 publication date), and a temporary population decline, eventually reaching a stationary level, Reddaway held that the basic problem was the maintenance of a high level of economic activity without the stimulus of population growth.[3]

A crucial point to Reddaway is the impact of a stationary population on the employment level. He anticipated that frictional unemployment would rise, since the population decline and eventual immobility would lengthen the economy's adjustment time. More important are the general level of unemployment and cyclical fluctuations. The argument is that barring voluntary or state-initiated changes in aggregate savings, the amount of capital outlay would be the key variable in determining the employment level. A declining or stationary population would probably induce a decline in capital formation by the private sector unless special measures were taken. Reddaway also noted that the level of capital outlay would be more sensitive to economic fluctuation than would be the case with a growing population. He contended that problems inherent in the maintenance of capital outlays are really attributable to man's lack of ingenuity in manipulating a particular economic system. In general, Reddaway concludes that population itself seldom dominates the economic situation; rather it renders problems of adjustment more or less difficult.

In a similar vein, Tsiang's (1942) long-term analysis suggested that a reduction in the scope for investment due to actual or imminent population decline would make it increasingly difficult to maintain full employment unless investment is stimulated or the propensity to save altered.[4] Furthermore, short-term analysis indicates that under these circumstances the economy would be more subject to fluctuation, with deeper depression, more difficult recovery, and lower peaks, due to the limits of labor supply.

Other writers also noted the impact of a decline in the population growth rate or a stationary population. Thompson (1939), writing about the United States, noted that with declining population growth, aggregate consumption would also grow at a lessened rate unless per capita consumption grew at a faster rate (than with a growing population).[5] Thompson pointed out that this was unlikely since the share of national income allocated to factors such as labor, return on capital, management and rent, which may have made for full employment and an increase in the standard of living under past conditions, are not automatically adjusted when the share of any one of these factors changes. The equilibrium is a highly unstable one in dynamic society.

In short, a change in the population growth rate induces a change in the effective demand for many varieties of producers and consumers goods and services. With the number of children declining as a population moves towards a stationary level, and with per capita income increasing, Thompson feels the standard of living will increase, the education of children will improve with lessened pressure on the educational system, and aggregate savings can be increased (as a share of total income). These savings, if large enough in the aggregate, can be used to produce luxuries to take up the slack caused by the decline in demand for necessities. Thompson adds that one way to increase effective per capita income without large population growth is through income redistribution.

On the role of savings, Leon Goldenberg (1946) tested empirically the impact on the size of savings of the relative stationarity of the French population from 1871 to 1911 relative to population changes in Germany and Great Britain. Goldenberg found that France had a lower proportion of national income invested at home than the other nations. Even considering this, France appeared to have relative capital abundance, as more than half was exported. This did not deter income growth in France but Goldenberg notes that ". . . there may be some doubt as to whether opportunities for safe foreign investment of excess capital would now be available . . ."

Baker (1937) made another attempt to evaluate the possible impact of a stationary population on the American economy. He thought such a population might be desirable in terms of the changed age structure and increased productivity which, ceteris paribus, would improve the standard of living. On the other hand, a declining population would have serious economic, social, and political ramifications.

Baker suggested five most probable bases for anticipating a continuing decline in fertility:

1. The experience of Great Britain, which had similar economic conditions, social ideals, and institutions, can be applied to the United States.

2. Historically, the highest U.S. birth rates have been (and still are) found among low income and rural people; Baker anticipated the fertility of these groups to decline in response to what may be loosely termed a demonstration effect.

3. Younger persons in the population have a lower ideal family size than did previous generations.

4. Due to the migration pattern (rural to urban) and its selectivity, the lower fertility of urban areas is apt to become more widespread.

5. Finally, via an echo effect, the low fertility of the present generation will limit the number of potential mothers in future generations.

Baker devotes considerable attention to the agricultural sphere and finds that a reduction in births, and consequently, a declining population, will have several effects.

1. The immediate fall in the number of children suggests a decline in the demand for agricultural products heavily consumed by them (milk is the most obvious example). In general, the per capita demand for agricultural products is relatively inelastic, so aggregate demand for agricultural products would probably decline, or cease growing.

2. With differential urban-rural fertility, population decline would be faster in urban areas, barring an acceleration of rural-urban migration. If the number of consumers of agricultural products declines at a rate greater than the number of producers and in the absence of an increase in per capita agricultural products, a less commercial agriculture will evolve.

3. The income distribution will become even more inequitous if most fertility declines occur among middle and upper income groups. Income is likely to be redistributed from rural to urban areas, since farm children will migrate in the absence of opportunity. When they inherit whatever their

farm-dwelling parents leave behind, the proceeds will follow them to the cities. Baker suggests that some of these problems could be avoided by the decentralization of the country, to encourage farm children to remain on the land. The ultimate solution, Baker feels, is replacing the spirit of selfishness so prevalent in capitalistic society with increased loyalty to the family.

The extent of the concern felt in the United States was reflected by the formation of the National Resources Committee (although the scope of the Committee went far beyond problems of population). The Committee's principal report (1938:2) dealing with population questions suggested that the advent of a stationary or declining population would open up new possibilities for ordered progress. The best land had already been taken, and diminishing returns had begun to set in in some extractive industries. A stationary population would permit continuation of a favorable man-resources ratio. The committee felt that ". . . future economic progress must be achieved for the most part by the conservation and better use of natural resources already tapped."

Spengler also made this point some years earlier (1933); he called the reliance on the discovery of new resources in major Western nations foolhardy. Spengler felt that reliance on new synthetic materials or technological advance only partially counteracted this. The rate of depletion of natural resources is positively related to the population growth rate, hence a slower or zero rate of population growth would ease much of the pressure on nonrenewable resources.

The National Resources Committee (1938:8) also felt that the anticipated decline in the population growth rate would not cause sudden economic disturbance since the population aged 20 to 45 would continue to increase for some time. Still, it noted that speculation on the economic future based on continued rapid population expansion would be hazardous and "continued expansion of the domestic market for American goods must be sought through the increase of effective consumer demand, through increased productivity and broadened distribution of income, rather than in numerical increase of population."

Writers in other nations were also concerned about the possible impact of a stationary population. Hurd (1939), for example, suggested that Canada was ". . . in the throes of adapting an economic structure geared to rapid population expansion in a situation where the population is growing at a materially and progressively slower rate." Wolstenholme (1936) made population projections for Australia showing that the maximum of eight to nine million would be reached sometime from 1977 to

1981. McCleary (1942) used Wolstenholme's results as the context for treatment of the problem by other Australian writers, most of whom suggested increased fertility as a means out of the dilemma. One notable exception was Duncan (1936 cited in McCleary 1942:32) who maintained that rapid increase in population could impair the high standard of living enjoyed by Australians and added that "Only the vulgar-minded confuse mere size with greatness. Australians may be genuinely patriotic . . . while admitting that our population will never increase."[6]

As a natural result of the concern with stationary or declining populations, many European governments adopted (or were urged to adopt) strong pro-natalist policies. Spengler (1951) has noted that in France immigration was promoted and a system of family allowances, while fairly generous, were insufficient to provide for all of a child's needs. One of the primary factors in this concern, as Spengler noted, was persistent fear of military domination. Harrod (1939), in noting the decline in fertility in the United Kingdom, advocated a system of children's allowances in each income class sufficient to place an economic premium on third and higher parity children.[7]

THE STAGNATION THESIS

As an adjunct to these arguments, it would seem logical to deduce that a decline in population growth might lead to circumstances most unfavorable to the continuation of economic growth. Indeed, the topic or possibility of economic decline received a great deal of attention when it appeared that the population of advanced nations might be approaching the stationary level or decline.

At this juncture, we would like to concentrate on an economic theory closely tied to the concept of stationary population (or to significant decline in the rate of population growth). Spengler (1959:808-09) summarized the major tenets of this theory, commonly termed the "stagnation thesis" as follows:

> Since a decline in R (rate of population growth) tends to be accompanied by a decline in the rate of investment and an increase in the rate of savings, investment will no longer suffice to offset savings under conditions of full employment. . . . Population growth, furthermore, is a dynamic and catalytic agent that makes for economic growth in general. Since a continually growing population insures a continually expanding market, entrepreneurs are not hesitant about investing in improved resource-saving equipment. . . .

Consequently, new and improved methods are introduced at a relatively high rate. Given that population growth has been so important a force of economic expansion and so significant a source of investment goods, it seemed to follow that a marked decline in the rate of population growth would result in a decline in technological progress, investment, and employment, with the multiplier effect and probably also the accelerator serving to intensify greatly the diminution of employment.

The amount of attention paid to this problem was quite large and many points in the argument were at times rather hotly disputed. Barber (1953), for example, has summarized the discussion in the relative significance of a declining rate of population growth and of a decline in the absolute numbers of increase. He notes that Hansen (1940,1946,1947,1954), Higgins (1946,1948), and Adler (1945), among others, hold that a falling percentage rate is a harbinger of a later decrease in absolute population size. Hansen particularly claims that this sets off a decline in investment, since the accelerator principle is based solely on absolute changes. Terborgh (1945,1946), on the other hand, likens the emphasis on absolute changes to the statement that a one pound increase in the weight of a dog is of equal significance to a one pound increase in the weight of an elephant.[8] Barber takes issue with Hansen saying that the accelerator principle applies to either relative or absolute change in population growth (or final demand, for that matter) and that the basic principle of the accelerator mechanism is that the ratio of income or consumption to capital is fixed.

The crux of the stagnationists' argument was that lack of population growth would lead to an insufficiency of aggregate demand and excess savings. Hansen (1941 and his earlier statement, 1939) argues that an increase in the absolute increment of population growth will lead to a redistribution of effective demand towards the purchase of investment goods (especially housing and expansion of public utilities), which, in turn would foster a higher level of output. Higgins (1950) adds that increased consumption may be expected to be at the expense of savings due to this income redistribution between wage earners and dependents. Peacock (1953-54) points out, however, that while an increase in population certainly implies an increase in need, it does not necessarily increase effective demand (see also Reddaway 1937).

In arguing against the stagnationists, Brockie (1950) feels that a primary problem might be industry's failure to adapt to the new-age industry due to institutional and organizational barriers. He also points out that some fears were due to population changes which appeared to him (in 1950) to be merely short-run phenomena. That is, the apparent stagnation in the economy may be due to a transitory, rather than permanent change in the population growth rate.

Other writers have also supplied counter arguments to various aspects of the thesis. Henderson (1938, cited by Brockie 1950), while he generally thought that the advantages of declining population were outweighed by disadvantages, held that a stationary or slowly growing population was more favorable in terms of welfare considerations than a rapidly growing population. Fellner (1946:55-70) denied that population growth would necessarily stimulate investment (via an increase in the marginal propensity to consume), noting that the *marginal* propensity of the old stock of population to consume was at least as great as the average propensity to consume of additional units of population.[9] Although Kuznets (1939) shows a negative relationship between investment and percentage change in population, Fellner (1941) claims that the data for the 1930s show no causal nexus between the simultaneous decline in investment and population growth. Peacock (1954) cites Jorgen Pederson (1948) to the effect that while an increase in population does imply an increase in the labor supply, there is no way for them to be absorbed in the absence of an increase in the demand for labor.

Finally, several writers have noted that only a relatively small increase in government spending (or consumption) would offset any loss in investment due to declining population growth, and that, in addition, investment with the United States continued to be quite high even after the rate of population increase began to decline (Spengler 1959:808).

CHANGING ATTITUDES AMONG ECONOMISTS

In conclusion, it is interesting to observe the changing attitude of the economics profession on the role of population growth and the change in relationship to economic growth. The termination of World War II was followed by a sizeable upturn in fertility in most Western nations, particularly the United States, due in part to the postponement of births during the war and perhaps to what Easterlin (1968:108ff.) calls an "unprecedented occurrence" of three circumstances favorable to family formation in the United States--a Kuznets-cycle economic expansion, restricted immigration, and a low rate of labor force entry by the native population resulting from demographic processes. The result was that most of the attention of the 1950s and 1960s concerned the probable effects of unabated population growth. An additional impetus to studies of this nature was provided by the emergence of newly independent nations during this period, many of which were hampered by severe population pressures.

The fertility decline which has accelerated in recent years is now beginning to be reflected in a renewal of interest in problems of declining or stationary populations. Studies of the Commission on Population Growth and the American Future (1972), Spengler (1971,1972), and others have generally reviewed the economic implications of these trends in a favorable light. Additionally, efforts by Mishan (1967), Daly (1972), and others have reflected favorably upon conditions of a stabilized economy. To date, there have been no new studies in the Keynes-Hansen tradition to complete the cycle of economic thought.

NOTES

1. See Spengler (1939); also Spengler (1938) which notes the trend in French thought on this subject tracing to the beginning of the fifteenth century. Also of interest in this regard is Caselot (1904) who notes that of all France, only Brittany was really "prolific" and noted the potential renewal of military problems with Germany, whose population was then increasing at a much faster rate.

2. Also of interest is Myrdal (1940). Myrdal feels that the overall impact of a population decline would hinge upon its magnitude and rapidity. The best outcome that can be anticipated, he claimed, for the West was a stationary population, even under the assumption of the most pro-natalistic policies. Myrdal felt then that population would become the dominant political and social problem in the world. Time has shown that this latter contention may still prove correct, although for quite different reasons than Myrdal proposed in 1940. See Myrdal (1968).

3. The second edition of this, published in 1946, shows that World War II and the increase in fertility experienced during and after the war did not invalidate, in general, most of Reddaway's conclusions.

4. Similar views appear in Sweezy (1940).

5. On the impact of declining population, see Spengler (1941).

6. A related article, Billing (1935), promotes increased immigration to Australia.

7. A more complete review of population policies of this period aimed at stimulating fertility appears in Glass (1936, 1940).

8. See also Wright's (1946) comment on the Hansen-Terborgh Dispute.

9. Fellner does add that population growth may favorably affect investment since ". . . the composition of the consumption of additional consuming units can be forecast . . . with less uncertainty than the composition of additional consumption of a given population" (1946:70). However, he adds that even with large population growth, a sizeable portion of increased consumption is due to per capita increases.

REFERENCES

Adler, H. A. (1945) "Absolute or Relative Decline in Population Growth." *Quarterly Journal of Economics* 59:626-34.

Baker, O. E. (1937) "Significance of Population Trends to American Agriculture." *Milbank Memorial Fund Quarterly* 15:121-34.

Barber, Clarence L. (1953) "Population Growth and the Demand for Capital." *American Economic Review* 43:133-39.

Billing, G. C. (1935) "Some Economic Effects of a Stationary Population." *Economic Record* 11:167-75.

Bowley, A. L. (1924) "Births and Population in Great Britain." *Economic Journal* 34:189-92.

Brockie, Melvin D. (1950) "Population Growth and the Rate of Investment." *Southern Economic Journal* 17:1-15.

Cannan, Edwin (1895) "The Probability of a Cessation of the Growth of Population in England and Wales During the Next Century." *Economic Journal* 5:505-15.

Caselot, Elvi (1904) "Stationary Population in France." *Economic Journal* 14:249-53.

Commission on Population Growth and the American Future (1972) *Population and the American Future*. Washington: U.S. Government Printing Office.

Daly, Herman. E (1972) "The Case for Zero Growth." *American Journal of Agricultural Economics* 54:945-54.

Duncan, W. G. K. (1936) "The Census and Migration," in *What the Census Means*, edited by G. V. Portus. Adelaide: F. W. Preece and Sons.

Easterlin, Richard A. (1968) *Population, Labor Force and Long Swings in Economic Growth*. New York: National Bureau of Economic Research.

Fellner, William John (1941) "The Technological Argument of the Stagnation Thesis." *Quarterly Journal of Economics* 55:638-51.

_____ (1946) *Monetary Policies and Full Employment*. Berkeley: University of California Press.

Glass, David V. (1936) *The Struggle for Population*. New York: Oxford University Press.

_____ (1940) *Population Policies and Movements in Europe*. 2d ed. New York: Kelly.

Goldenberg, Leon (1946) "Savings in a State with a Stationary Population." *Quarterly Journal of Economics* 61:40-65.

Hansen, Alvin H. (1939) "Economic Progress and Declining Population Growth." *American Economic Review* 29:1-15.

_____ (1940) "Extensive Expansion and Population Growth." *Journal of Political Economy* 48:583-85.

_____ (1941) *Fiscal Policy and Business Cycles*. New York: Norton.

_____ (1946) "Some Notes on Terborgh's *The Bogey of Economic Maturity*." *Review of Economics and Statistics* 28:13-14.

_____ (1947) *Economic Policy and Full Employment*. New York: McGraw-Hill.

_____ (1954) "Growth or Stagnation in the American Economy." *Review of Economics and Statistics* 36:409-14.

Harrod, R. F. (1934) "Modern Population Trends." *Manchester School* 1:1-21.

Henderson, H. E. (1938) "Economic Consequences," in Marshall et al., *The Population Problem*.

Higgins, Benjamin H. (1946) "The Doctrine of Economic Maturity." *American Economic Review* 36:133-41.

_____ (1948) "Concepts and Criteria of Secular Stagnation," in *Income, Employment and Public Policy: Essays in Honor of Alvin H. Hansen*, by Lloyd A. Metzler et al. New York: Norton.

_____ (1950) "The Theory of Increasing Underemployment." *Economic Journal* 60:255-74.

Hurd, W. Burton (1939) "Some Implications of Prospective Population Changes in Canada." *Canadian Journal of Economics and Political Science* 5:492-503.

Keynes, John Maynard (1937) "Some Economic Consequences of a Declining Population." *Eugenics Review* 29:13-17.

Kuczynski, Robert René (1928) *Western and Northern Europe. The Balance of Births and Deaths*, vol. 1. Institute of Economics of the Brookings Institution. Publication 29, 43. New York: Macmillan.

―――― (1931) *Eastern and Southern Europe. The Balance of Births and Deaths*, vol. 2. Washington, D.C.: The Brookings Institution.

―――― (1938) "World Population," in Marshall, et al., *The Population Problem*.

Kuznets, Simon (1939) "Capital Formation in the United States, 1919-1935," in *Capital Formation and Its Elements*. New York: National Industrial Conference Board.

Lafitte, F. (1940) "The Economic Effects of a Declining Population." *Eugenics Review* 32:121-34.

Marshall, Thomas Humphrey et al., eds. (1938) *The Population Problem: The Experts and the Public*. London: Allen and Unwin.

McCleary, G. F. (1942) "Australia's Population Problem." *Milbank Memorial Fund Quarterly* 20:23-34.

Mishan, Edward J. (1967) *The Costs of Economic Growth*. New York: Praeger.

Myrdal, Gunnar (1940) *Population: A Problem for Democracy*. Cambridge, Mass.: Harvard University Press.

―――― (1968) *Asian Drama: An Inquiry into the Poverty of Nations*. New York: Twentieth Century Fund.

National Resources Committee (1938) *The Problem of a Changing Population*. Washington: U.S. Government Printing Office.

Neisser, Hans (1944) "The Economics of a Stationary Population." *Social Research* 11:476-90.

Peacock, Alan T. (1953-54) "Theory of Population and Modern Economic Analysis." *Population Studies* 6:114-22; 7:227-34.

Pederson, Jorgen (1948) "Interest Rates, Employment, and Changes in Population." *Kyklos* 2:1-15.

Reddaway, William Brian (1937) "Special Obstacles to Full Employment." *Economic Journal* 47:297-307.

_____ (1946) *The Economics of a Declining Population*. 2d ed. New York: Macmillan.

Robbins, Lionel (1929) "Notes on Some Probable Consequences of the Advent of Stationary Population in Great Britain." *Economica* 9:71-82.

Spengler, Joseph J. (1933) "The Social and Economic Consequences of Cessation in Population Growth." *Proceedings of the International Congress for Studies on Population* 9:33-60.

_____ (1938) *France Faces Depopulation*. Durham, N.C.: Duke University Press.

_____ (1939) "Moheau: Prophet of Depopulation." *Journal of Political Economy* 47:648-77.

_____ (1941) "Population Trends and the Future Demand for Teachers." *Social Forces* 19:467-76.

_____ (1951) "Notes on France's Response to Her Declining Rate of Demographic Growth." *Journal of Economic History* 11:403-16.

_____ (1959) "Economics and Demography," in *The Study of Population*, edited by Philip M. Hauser and Otis D. Duncan. Chicago: University of Chicago Press.

_____ (1971) *Declining Population Growth Revisited*. Monograph 14. Chapel Hill: Carolina Population Center, The University of North Carolina at Chapel Hill.

_____ (1972) "Prospective Population Changes and Price Level Tendencies." *Southern Economic Journal* 38:459-67.

Staudinger, Hans (1936) "Stationary Population--Stagnant Economy?" *Social Research* 6:141-53.

Sweezy, Alan R. (1940) "Population Growth and Investment Opportunities." *Quarterly Journal of Economics* 55:64-79.

Terborgh, George (1945) *The Bogey of Economic Maturity*. Chicago: Machinery and Allied Products Institute.

_____ (1946) "Dr. Hansen on *The Bogey of Economic Maturity*." *Review of Economics and Statistics* 28:170-72.

Thompson, Warren S. (1939) "The Economic Consequences of Slow Population Growth in the United States," in *Proceedings of the Ohio Conference of Statisticians on Business Research*. Columbus: Ohio State University Press.

Tsiang, S. C. (1942) "The Effect of Population Growth on the General Level of Employment and Activity." *Economica* 9 (NS):325-32.

Weiner, Myron (1971) "Political Demography," in *Rapid Population Growth: Consequences and Policy Implications*, edited by Roger Revell. Baltimore: The Johns Hopkins Press.

Wolfe, A. B. (1928) "The Population Problem Since the World War: A Survey of Literature and Research." *Journal of Political Economy* 36:529-59; 662-85; 37:87-120.

Wolstenholme, S. H. (1936) "The Future of the Australian Population." *Economic Record* 12:195-213.

Wright, David McC. (1946) "The Great Guessing Game: Terborgh vs. Hansen." *Review of Economics and Statistics* 28:18-22.

3

The Natural History of the Stagnation Thesis

ALAN R. SWEEZY

The term *secular stagnation* is really a misnomer. What Keynes, Hansen, and the other "stagnationists" of the 1930s were worried about was not that technological progress would cease and productivity stagnate but rather that the flow of investment expenditure might be inadequate over extended periods of time to maintain reasonably full employment of labor and other resources.

The theoretical underpinnings of the stagnation thesis are found in the Keynesian theory of income and employment and in the neoclassical theory of capital. Income theory explains why investment expenditure is important; capital theory, why it might be inadequate. Investment plays a key role in Keynesian income theory because the theory assumes that the community's consumption-saving pattern is inflexible and that there is a positive level of interest rates below which investors will prefer to hold money rather than to acquire real capital goods. Hence, as investment spending falls, the result might be, not a shift from the production of capital to the production of consumer goods as in classical theory, but an overall decline in spending and with it a drop in output and employment.

Neoclassical capital theory distinguishes three ways in which capital can be profitably invested:

1. In outfitting additional workers with equipment of the same type already being used—it will not pay, however, to build such equipment unless there *are* additional workers to operate it

2. In increasing the amount of capital per worker within the range of already known technological possibilities

3. In introducing new technology and developing new resources.

Investment of type 2 is subject to the law of diminishing returns: as more capital is added to a given amount of labor its marginal product, and hence its profitability, declines. Any reduction in the opportunities for investment of types 1 or 3 would, unless the rate of accumulation also drops, force more capital into type 2 and thus bring the rate of return down below what it would otherwise be. Opportunities for type 1 investment depend on the increase in the labor force which, in turn, in the long run depends on the growth of population.

Until the 1930s interest in the problems of unemployment and reduced output was confined to short-run fluctuations in economic activity, the so-called business cycle. As the depression wore on, however, its unprecedented severity and length gave rise to a growing suspicion that something more serious than the ordinary down-phase of the business cycle was involved. Many people of liberal or radical bent were inclined to think that the whole private ownership, market-oriented economic system had broken down and would have to be replaced by some kind of planned economy. They were vague as to what exactly this would entail or how it could be brought about.

Keynes took a different tack. Influenced no doubt by the unsatisfactory performance of the British economy in the 1920s, he had already begun speculating before the mid-1930s about the possibility that basic changes were occurring in the opportunities for profitable investment of capital.

> The post-war experiences of Great Britain and the United States are indeed examples of how an accumulation of wealth, so large that its marginal efficiency has fallen more rapidly than the rate of interest can fall in the face of the prevailing institutional factors, can interfere, in conditions mainly of *laissez-faire*, with a reasonable level of employment and with the standard of life which the technical conditions of production are capable of furnishing (Keynes 1936:219).

He was joined in these speculations by Hansen and many of the younger American Keynesians after private investment had failed to rise as expected in the short-lived recovery of 1937-38. This change in focus from the unplanned nature of the economy to a possible deficiency of investment demand had profound policy implications: it opened up the prospect that the persistent malaise of the thirties could be cured without abandoning the private ownership, market-directed economy itself.

As they thought about the long-run determinants of investment demand, the stagnationists came inevitably--being trained in neoclassical theory as they were--to focus their attention on population growth and the territorial expansion which in the nineteenth century had accompanied it and given it immunity from the Law of Diminishing Returns. Both Keynes and Hansen estimated that a large part of investment, perhaps as much as one-half, in the century preceding World War I had been associated with population growth. But population growth in the Western world was slowing down and would soon cease. With the slow-down, investment opportunities would be relatively smaller than they had been in the past and unless appropriate policy changes were made, we would see a chronic tendency to low income and underemployment of resources. This in brief was the stagnation thesis.

CRITICISMS OF THE STAGNATION THEORY

The thesis has been subjected to three broadly different types of criticism: the first is a product of misunderstanding; the second reflects dissatisfaction with the theory of investment demand, especially as concerns the role of population growth; the third consists of an appeal to the facts of economic life since World War II.

Misunderstanding of the Term Stagnation

Misunderstanding is in large part attributable to the misleading connotations of the term *secular stagnation*. The term implies a cessation of economic progress, literally a stagnation of economic activity of all types. That is not at all what Keynes, Hansen, and their followers had in mind. They repeatedly stated their conviction that technological change would continue and that productivity would go on increasing. Nor did they think, as is often alleged, that we had reached a condition of capital saturation, that there would be "no more" investment opportunities. They thought that not only technological progress but also the investment associated with it would continue. Their thesis was simply that with declining population growth one important class of investment outlets was disappearing. They were skeptical that technological progress would become so much more rapid as to make up for the loss.

Dissatisfaction with the Theory of Investment Demand

The second type of criticism stems from readily understandable dissatisfaction with the theory of investment demand. It is clear how population growth fits into the long-run theory of capital. As already indicated, the more capital is combined with a given amount of labor--assuming either constant technology or a constant rate of technological change--the lower the rate of return on capital will be. It follows that if the growth of population and the labor supply decreases, while capital accumulation continues unabated, the rate of return on capital will decline. Moving from capital to Keynesian income theory, it seems logical to conclude that if the fall is drastic enough it will reach the point at which investors prefer to hold money and an overall decline in spending will ensue. We thus have the paradoxical result that a lower rate of increase of the labor supply could cause unemployment.

There are difficulties, however, in tracing through this analysis in detail. The reason a decline in population growth causes a drop in profit presumably is that employers, bidding against each other for the more limited supply of labor, force wages up and profits down. This assumes prices are unaffected by the rise of wages. Here we run into trouble, however, with Keynesian theory. Joan Robinson (1942) states the Keynesian objection to the classical theory on this point in her *Essay on Marxian Economics*. Marx, reasoning along classical lines, held that "at some periods the stock of capital, which governs the amount of employment offered, catches up with the supply of labour--real wages tend to rise and profits consequently fall." Mrs. Robinson (1942:100) objects on the ground that "an equal proportional rise in all money wages must lead to the same proportional rise in the level of prices," leaving profits unchanged.

A similar problem arises when we try to trace the effects of a decline of population growth into the period of depression which follows the initial drop in spending and employment. If more labor helped to maintain profits and hence investment in a period of expansion, why would not the existence of unemployed labor have the same effect in a period of depression? In other words, why does a depression not cure itself as soon as unemployment appears?

Leaving these questions unanswered, economists have chosen either to ignore population growth entirely in their analysis of the determinants of income and employment or to concentrate on a different aspect of the relationship, namely, the effect of population growth on consumer spending and saving. Most of them seem to be unaware that labor supply could have anything to do with the problem.

Gardner Ackley (1961), for example, criticizes Keynes and Hansen for not seeing that even without population growth, expansion of income could provide a *market* for the product of a growing stock of capital.

> We have already considered the basic error of this Keynesian position. It is a failure to realize that a growth of income can prevent capital saturation. . . . An economy twice as big in annual output can use twice as much capital (Ackley 1961:511).

What Ackley fails to explain is how it would be possible to operate twice as much capital of the same kinds--we are abstracting here from technological change, assuming that its rate is unaffected by the change in population growth--without more labor. John Cornwall (1972) and Allen Kelley (1972) likewise ignore the relation between labor supply and capital stock, confining their analysis to saving and spending on consumer durable goods. Even Hansen, though he stressed the importance of "capital widening," defined widening in relation to *output* instead of to labor supply. He thus left himself exposed to Ackley's criticism.

As to consumer demand, both Hansen and Cornwall think the effect of population growth is likely to be favorable; favorable, that is, in an economy which may have difficulty maintaining an adequate flow of demand. Cornwall elaborates Hansen's argument but his main points are essentially the same. He assumes that the propensity to spend on nondurables and services is unaffected by population growth but that "family related" expenditures (housing and other consumer durables) would be larger with a growing population. He also thinks the pressure to borrow is greater for couples making first purchases of consumer durables--especially housing--than for other types of consumers. Kelley's exhaustive survey of the theoretical and empirical literature on saving, provides little positive support for Cornwall's conclusion, but also no reason for rejecting it.

The implications of the stagnation thesis are not necessarily pessimistic, as they are usually depicted. Leijonhufvud (1968: 411), for instance, says: "Keynes looked forward to an indefinite period of, at best, unrelenting deflationary pressure . . . [which] he painted in colors not many shades brighter than the gloomy hues of the stagnationist picture." Leijonhufvud, incidentally, always tries to make a distinction between Keynes' ideas and those of his simple-minded American followers. To paint the stagnation thesis as pessimistic in its implications for the economic future is to miss the essential point. Keynes, Hansen, and their followers called attention to the effect of declining population growth on investment expenditure in order to strengthen the case for an active fiscal and monetary policy. Given such a policy it would be easy to compensate for any deficiency in investment demand, whether temporary or chronic, by increasing public expenditure, shifting the propensity to consume, or lowering interest rates.

Given an active fiscal and monetary policy, the implications of the stagnation thesis are actually highly optimistic. For any easing of the pressure of private demand on available resources opens the way for more adequate satisfaction of social and environmental needs. This was less obvious in the thirties than it is now, but even then many liberals were beginning to feel that increased government spending was desirable not only as an offset to inadequate private investment spending but also for the benefit it would bring society. Although no one had expressed the idea with the force and clarity of Galbraith's *Affluent Society* (1958), there was a growing feeling that the public sector had been neglected and that it was high time to redress the balance.

*Dissatisfaction with the Economic
Predictions of the Stagnation Theory*

The third type of criticism of the stagnation thesis is that things have not turned out the way it predicted they would. Instead of chronic unemployment and deflation, we have had high employment and inflation most of the time in most of the Western world since the 1930s. In part, at least, this criticism is also based on misunderstanding. The stagnation thesis was not so much a prediction of what *would* actually happen as a warning of what *could* happen if certain far-reaching policy changes were not made. The changes have been made and have had an important influence on the course of events. In other ways, too, the postwar world has been very different from the world of the twenties and thirties. Most important for the present discussion, the government sector of the economy in the West, as a result both of war and of increased assumption of social responsibilities, has been a much larger part of the whole than in the past. This has greatly reduced dependence on the flow of private investment spending in maintaining prosperity and high employment.

THE POSTWAR ECONOMIC PICTURE

There was, of course, plenty of reason to be worried about a deficiency of aggregate demand in the 1930s. Then for a while in the late fifties and early sixties in the United States it seemed that the problem might, at least in modified form, be returning. For several years investment remained low as a fraction of income, growth slowed down, and unemployment persisted in the 5.5 to 7 percent range. Dernburg and McDougall (1966), writing in the mid-sixties, thought the danger of stagnation was still real:

> Perhaps as a result of World War II and the conditions that attended its aftermath, the American economy's principal problem over the years 1940-1955 was quite the opposite of the problem that concerned Hansen. Instead of deficient aggregate demand, demand was in excess of what the economy could supply, with the result that we suffered inflationary pressures during the period. However, beginning in 1957, the economy reverted for a period of seven years to secular stagnation marked by excessive unemployment and a slow rate of growth. Hansen's analysis now appears to be not nearly as obsolete as its detractors thought it to be. Stagnation of the deficient demand variety is an ever-present danger that the economy must be ever ready to guard against (Dernburg and McDougall 1966:293).

A palatable remedy was ready to hand. With the Federal budget accounting for approximately 16 percent of gross national income as compared with only 3 percent in the late 1920s, changes in tax rates had become a potentially powerful instrument for influencing the rate of economic activity. After much soul-searching and debate and an intensive educational campaign led by Walter Heller and his colleagues on the Council of Economic Advisers, the government and the public were persuaded to accept a massive tax cut as a means of increasing income, production, and employment. The "fiscal drag" which had been holding expansion back was removed and even before the stimulus of the Vietnam war began to be felt, the economy was moving on to a more satisfactory level of activity.

Since the mid-sixties further changes have occurred in the American economy. Most important is the increase in the *civilian* expenditures of the federal government. The Brookings economists in their review of the budgetary situation early in 1973 pointed out that civilian expenditures had almost doubled from the mid-sixties to the early seventies. As a result "the annual growth in *existing* expenditure programs now absorbs a much larger fraction of the growth in revenues than was the case ten years ago" (Schultze et al. 1973:398). Moreover "the American people and their political representatives have accepted a greatly broadened concept of the appropriate role of the federal government in dealing with the nation's social problems; there is a large backlog of unmet demands for new or sharply expanded federal programs addressed to those problems--assuming a share of the burden of local educational finance, providing day care centers for children of working mothers, and financing a large part of the cost of environmental cleanup, to name but a few." As a result the nature of the budgetary problem has been radically changed. The historical problem of fiscal drag--the tendency for increases in tax receipts to outrun increases in expenditures--has been transformed into its opposite, the problem of "fiscal squeeze." With this change there is little prospect that we will have to be concerned with a deficiency of aggregate demand for a long time to come.

POPULATION GROWTH AND THE ECONOMY

Although we still do not fully understand the way in which population growth affects investment, and hence income and employment, it is probable that the stagnationists were right in thinking that, under favorable circumstances such as those which existed in the nineteenth century, population growth has a stimulating effect on investment. It does not at all follow, however, that we should encourage population growth as a way of insuring a high level of income and employment. Not only are other means of accomplishing this objective available, the environmental and resource implications of continued population growth are quite unacceptable.

The stagnationists of the 1930s were in complete agreement with this conclusion. In his Presidential address to the American Economic Association Hansen said: "Schooled in the traditions of Malthusian theory, economists have typically placed an optimistic interpretation upon the cessation of population growth. . . . In a fundamental sense this conclusion is, I think, thoroughly sound." He warned that there may, however, be "in the current drastic shift from rapid expansion to cessation of population growth serious structural maladjustments which can be avoided only if economic policies, appropriate to the changed situation are applied" (Hansen 1939:2).

Keynes is even more emphatic in underlining his adherence to Malthusian doctrine. He concluded his Eugenics Society lecture by reassuring his audience:

> But if there are any old Malthusians here present let them not suppose that I am rejecting their essential argument. Unquestionably a stationary population does facilitate a rising standard of life; but on one condition only--namely, that the increase in resources or in

consumption which the stationariness of population makes possible, does actually take place. For we have learned that we have another devil at our elbow at least as fierce as the Malthusian--namely the devil of unemployment escaping through the breakdown of effective demand. . . . When devil P of Population is chained up, we are free of one menace; but we are more exposed to the other devil U of Unemployed Resources than we were before (Keynes 1937:131-32).

Today the Malthusian devil P, though coming under control in the developed countries, still roams freely in most of the rest of the world. His counterpart U, whose depredations in the developed countries Keynes feared, is securely chained up, thanks in large measure to the improved understanding of how to manage our economic affairs we owe to Keynes himself.

REFERENCES

Ackley, Gardner (1961) *Macroeconomic Theory*. New York: Macmillan.

Cornwall, John (1972) *Growth and Stability in a Mature Economy*. New York: Wiley.

Dernburg, Thomas F. and McDougall, Duncan M. (1966) *Macroeconomics: The Measurement, Analysis, and Control of Aggregate Economic Activity*. New York: McGraw-Hill.

Galbraith, John Kenneth (1958) *The Affluent Society*. Boston: Houghton Mifflin.

Hansen, Alvin H. (1939) "Economic Progress and Declining Population Growth." *American Economic Review* 29:1-15.

_____ (1941) *Fiscal Policy and Business Cycles*. New York: Norton.

Kelley, Allen C. (1972) "Demographic Changes and American Economic Development: Past, Present and Future," in *Economic Aspects of Population Change,* edited by Elliott R. Morss and Ritchie H. Reed, Commission on Population Growth and the American Future Research Reports, vol. 2. Washington: U.S. Government Printing Office.

Keynes, John Maynard (1936) *The General Theory of Employment, Interest and Money*. London: Macmillan & Co., Ltd.

_____ (1937) "Some Economic Consequences of a Declining Population." *Eugenics Review* 29:13-17.

Leijonhufvud, Axel (1968) *On Keynesian Economics and the Economics of Keynes: A Study in Monetary Theory*. New York: Oxford University Press.

Robinson, Joan (1942) *Essay on Marxian Economics*. London: Macmillan & Co., Ltd.

Schultze, Charles L.; Fried, Edward R.; Rivlin, Alice M.; and Teeters, Nancy H. (1972) *Setting National Priorities: The 1973 Budget*. Washington: The Brookings Institution.

4

Higher Education in the Stationary Population: A Comment on North Carolina's System

V. JEFFREY EVANS

Higher education has long been a point of pride in North Carolina, and currently, it is a leading industry in the state economy as well as a key point of contention in intrastate regional rivalry. At present, there are 45 senior institutions and 77 community colleges and technical institutes--which are, in part, college parallel (Taylor 1972). At the senior level, there is a strong core of state supported institutions composed of many regional campuses joined under the direction of the Board of Governors of the University of North Carolina and a fringe of private institutions, mostly church related. Some of the private institutions are large universities which can stand alone and prosper but most are small, liberal arts colleges which depend heavily on tuition for survival. Community colleges and technical institutes have grown rapidly in recent years and most are heavily subsidized by the state. There are, however, some private church-related junior colleges. In sum, 122 institutions are competing for the attention of prospective students.

Geographically, the competition is severe. In both rural and urban areas, public and private four- and two-year institutions try to coexist in the face of ever increasing competition. For instance, the Greensboro/Winston-Salem/High Point area has four state supported universities, seven private colleges, four Bible colleges, three technical institutes, and one private junior college (Taylor 1972). In many rural areas, the competition is just as keen and, in fact, state support for community colleges in these areas is growing.

What then does this imply? The trend is in the direction of

intense competition among institutions for students who are the base of survival and power. This kind of competition also implies that there will be casualties as the "crunch" gathers momentum. Who will be the casualties? When and where will they occur? Is this event in the best interest of the state? What can be done about it? These questions form the basis of this inquiry. Further, I suggest that the casualties will be the private institutions in the very near future and that it is in the best interest of the state to forestall this calamity.

The central thesis of this inquiry is that in certain instances the state has legitimate reasons for intervening in operation of higher education to suppress self-destructive tendencies. Moreover, the certain contingencies mentioned above are related to the expected demographic and economic future of North Carolina specifically and the United States generally; and these contingencies demand that public, educational planning incorporate considerable flexibility in capacity. I will first outline the demographic and economic outlook for the near future and then examine what hazards these trends present to the planner. Next, we will discover why the present system of educational planning may not provide any of the answers to this problem which, in turn, implies public intervention. Finally, the formulation and implementation of public policy is discussed.

THE DEMOGRAPHIC OUTLOOK

The size and composition of a population is determined by the factors of fertility, mortality, and migration. Fertility has been the most volatile parameter nationally and recently fell below the replacement level. In fact, the "baby boom" has turned into a "baby bust." The ramification of this event will be reflected in population growth for generations to come. Figure 4.1 depicts the typical result of such a fertility decrease.

If we assume that fertility levels will hover around the replacement level (implying that the population will eventually stabilize at a zero growth rate), then the total population and every age group within the age structure will grow in a damped oscilliatory pattern until it eventually stabilizes at a fixed growth rate--ideally, a zero growth rate (Keyfitz 1968). The period of the oscillation is roughly that of a generation and present trends indicate that we have two or three generations of rapid change ahead of us. The population should stabilize at some fixed number which should be approximately 40-50 percent greater than the present population. Please note, however, that there will be times when the population is greater than the

stable population and also times when it is less. If we plan
for a stable population, obviously we should not overlook the
periods of fluctuation.

Figure 4.1. Growth-Path of a Typical Stationary Population

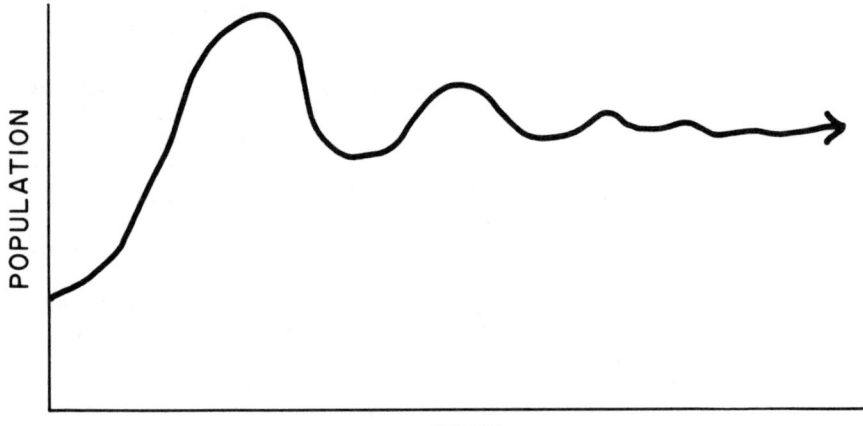

Any age group within the population will exhibit similar behavior but on a different time schedule. Younger groups will experience a change before older groups. The plight of elementary education signals the future trends for higher education and such a drama will definitely unfold since the actors are already on stage. Figure 4.2 charts the projected change in the 20-24 age category for North Carolina from 1970 to 2000.

The 20-24 age group was chosen because it is a strong proxy for the age group who go to college, and the 30-year period is the foreseeable future and, consequently, the planning horizon. But this is just the first stage of a multistage transition, as described above. As we can see, the population of this age group will still grow until 1985 but will fall rapidly thereafter. This means that we could blind ourselves to the grim reality of demographic processes for another dozen years if we so desire, but the final reckoning is inevitable.

There are factors which can partially alleviate these circumstances. Migration can and probably will bring people, young people, into the state of North Carolina. Migration decreases the magnitude of the fluctuation but the pattern of oscillation is still there (Evans 1972). It is also possible that the propensity to go to college may increase, but research shows that this would only delay the inevitable by 5-8 years (Evans 1972). In short, demographic change must be confronted by the educational establishment.

Figure 4.2. Number of 20-24 Year Olds--North Carolina, 1965-2000

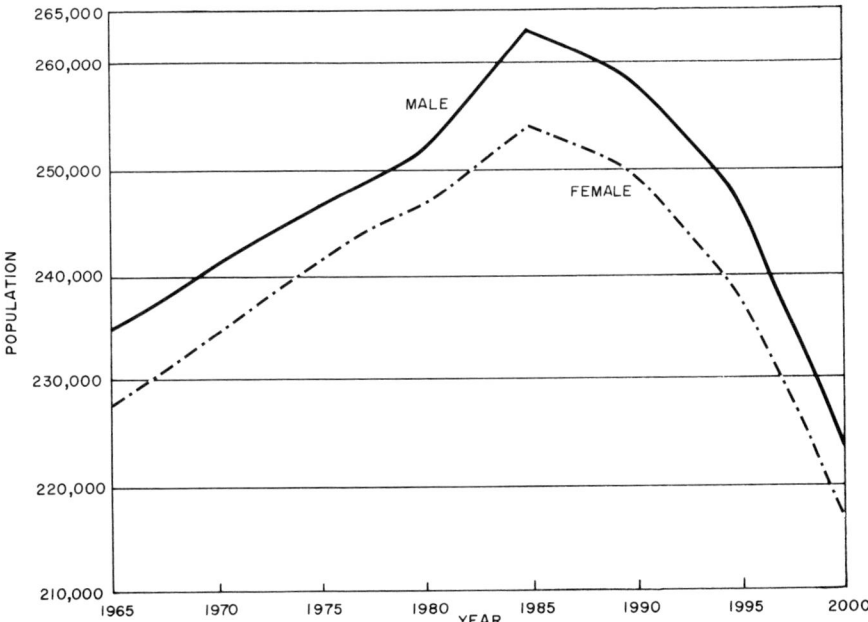

THE ECONOMIC OUTLOOK

From an economic viewpoint, there are at least two ways of analysing higher education. First, the interests of society at large must be investigated to ascertain the proper priority of higher education in the public interest and to determine whether the institution is meeting the expectations attendant to that priority. Second, a microeconomic examination of higher education is needed to discover why the individual demands education and how these demands are likely to change in the stationary population. Combine the two analyses and an outline of the outside economic pressures on the institution emerges. The question of internal institutional response to these pressures is a totally different problem and is discussed only briefly.

The Interests of Society

The accumulation of human capital in the form of college graduates is a legitimate item of public interest. No matter if it is in the form of public or of private education, the end product does have a significant and positive impact on society. It is, therefore, in the public interest to ensure the efficient operation of the industry.

Increasing the stock of human capital through education serves society in an immediate sense by increasing the quality of the labor force which, in turn, increases the productivity of labor. This is a necessary prerequisite for increasing the level of economic welfare in society. Also since the industrial structure is rapidly changing from one dominated by the primary concerns of heavy industry to one characterized by more secondary concerns, such as the service industries, an efficient educational structure is necessary for such a transition to take place. Human capital is also a mode of social mobility, and if higher education falters, the expectations of many minority groups may not materialize. Clearly, society has come too far to tolerate such a condition.

Finally, the long-run goal is to increase the overall welfare of society. We are on the brink of solving problems of material welfare, and eventually, we can guarantee a goodly amount of leisure to every citizen. All will be for naught if society does not develop sufficient stocks of human capital to sustain a cultural advance commensurate with expected material progress. What could be more futile than to allow centuries of material progress go unappreciated for a lack of education? Certainly, society expects our educational frontiers to expand.

Any individual within society makes similar demands on higher education. He has two basic motivations for demanding more education: (1) it is an investment in his future and (2) it has a consumption value in itself. In the recent past, pressures for material security and the avalanche of reproductive activity following World War II have emphasized the investment part of higher education and largely ignored the consumption aspects. This is a proper reaction to an expanding population. Society, in this case, is preoccupied with the welfare of the young since they are the hope for the future and they numerically dominate society. However, the sun has begun to set on the justifications for such an investment priority and a new dawn is arriving.

The sun will rise on a stationary population with a more mature taste in educational priority. Society will demand education as much for its consumption value as for its investment potential. Education will be for the young and *old*, and it will be as much part time as full time. Moreover, it is quite likely that the emphasis on degrees per se will be considerably modified not only in the subject matter covered but also in importance as a rationale for study.

The Price and Income Effects

Aside from basic economic motivations, there are two immediate stimuli which determine whether or not a student will enter higher education: (1) the relative price of education and (2) the level of income.

Education is an industry which encompasses many diverse programs varying in type and quality. For each class of programs, the ones with the lower price will attract more students. This is called the *price effect*.

Moreover, as the level of income increases, two options open for the consumer. First, he can consume more education, and certainly this is the case in North Carolina and in the country generally. Second, he may elect to consume not more but better, higher quality education. The exercise of these two options is called the *income effect,* and since income levels will certainly double and maybe triple before the end of the century, one may expect the income effect to dominate the scene.

Taken together, the price effect and the income effect in the circumstance of the stationary population may mean that more people will demand a better education. Consequently, low-cost youth-oriented degree mills may be dinosaurs of the twentieth century.

PROBLEMS FOR THE EDUCATIONAL PLANNER

As the population stabilizes, the educational planner faces two considerable problems. He must, first, avoid accumulating more capacity than the future requires while maintaining sufficient flexibility to accommodate the "ups and downs" of population growth. Also, he must be sure that there is a proper mix of program, that the quality is at the desired level and that the programs are distributed in such a way that they are accessible to future populations. The matter is further complicated by the fact that there are, at least, four competing interest groups which must be coordinated: (1) local authorities within a state; (2) state authorities; (3) federal authorities; and (4) a substantial private sector, divided into a myriad of church-related interest and into nonsectarian institutions.

Each sphere of influence plans from a different perspective, but all approaches have one common characteristic: they plan by virtue of hindsight. This particular analytic framework has a few remarkable disadvantages which figure 4.3 illustrates.

Population is plotted versus time and the oscillatory line depicts a typical population growth curve as it damps out into a stationary population. Arrow 1 indicates the intrinsic rate of natural increase which is the rate at which the stable population grows and, in the case of a stationary population, the growth rate is zero at a given level of population.

In the long run, society only needs an educational structure sufficient to support a population of a size represented by arrow 1, but the long run is three generations, 75 years, into the future. What shall we use as our guide in the interim period? Moreover, to invest in higher education means that society must forego other social objectives, and to overinvest in education means that society must underinvest in other areas. Further, if society underinvests in education and if education is a prime input for continued progress in other areas, which is certainly true, then education becomes a bottleneck and progress in a wide range of other activities will be much less than it could have been. Following are several planning approaches which either have been or can be used to implement proper policy.

PLANNING TO IMPLEMENT POLICY

The best approach is to formulate a long-run plan calculated to ride the waves of social change into the stable population. In North Carolina, the Board of Higher Education attempted to do that for years but the many practical problems attendant to the approach eventually crushed the office and gives good witness to the suspicion that the approach is practically impossible. The first difficulty is that there are many external influences which can wreck momentary havoc with enrollment projections. Changes in migration patterns, economic boom and depression, war, and transitory changes in natural parameters within the population can produce a temporary reality much different from the projected. Also, it is practically impossible to induce all of the spheres of influence to move in one direction. For instance, the federal government has for the past 15 years encouraged expansion with massive aid and now is causing sudden contraction by withdrawing its aid. The private sector has steadfastly refused to do any planning while the state system is in danger of succumbing to the rampant regionalism of political jealousy. Even individual counties seem to be in a race to build community colleges and technical institutes. What is needed is a flexible plan which is politically tractable.

The current approach seems to be opportunistic which means that one rides the current trend and hopes for the best. Simply calculate the past trend, extrapolate it into the future, and race to capture the momentum of the hour. While this approach has a "gut" appeal and may even work for an individual institution, it has the drawback that the system is always wrong and there is always considerable danger of an emotional overreaction sufficient to bring the system to the brink of destruction.

Consider figure 4.3. Points A and C are possible situations and if the recent past is extrapolated into the future, as arrows 2 and 3 suggest, the educational structure can end up massively overextended or hopelessly undercapitalized depending on how firm the planners are in their conviction that the approach is solid. Moreover, since educational plans take years to complete, once a plan is implemented, society is stuck with it for many years into the future. In short, the approach has the drawback of always being out of phase with reality by 5-10 years, and it also is susceptible to the possibility that we may be blinded by rapidly rising or rapidly falling enrollments so as to overreact by heroic proportions.

Estimating Labor's Natural Growth Rate

There is an approach which may work. It combines the "turnpike" theorem (Kemeny, Morganstern, and Thompson 1956) with time honored devices for market stabilization. It addresses itself to the problems of economic efficiency in accumulating social overhead capital, of economic flexibility, and of the difficulty of coordinating different spheres of authority. The first issue of economic efficiency should be the prime concern of any plan. We must find a way of accumulating social overhead capital in such a way as to ensure that there are no bottlenecks. Elimination of bottlenecks is important since socioeconomic progress can only proceed as fast as the scarcest factor accumulates. Moreover, in the long run labor is the key factor and actually as the socioeconomic system stabilizes in the stationary population, labor's growth rate dominates all (Solow 1956). Therefore, estimating the long-run growth rate of the labor force--the so-called natural growth rate--is our first concern.

A good approximation of the natural growth rate in the stationary population is the intrinsic rate of natural increase (arrow 1 in figure 4.3). As long as planning is done according to the intrinsic rate, the plan will never be wrong by much and as the population stabilizes, the plan becomes more accurate which is in marked contrast with the increasing error of the approaches discussed above. How do we incorporate such a device as the intrinsic rate into a plan?

Figure 4.3. The Intrinsic Rate of Natural Increase as a Planning Parameter

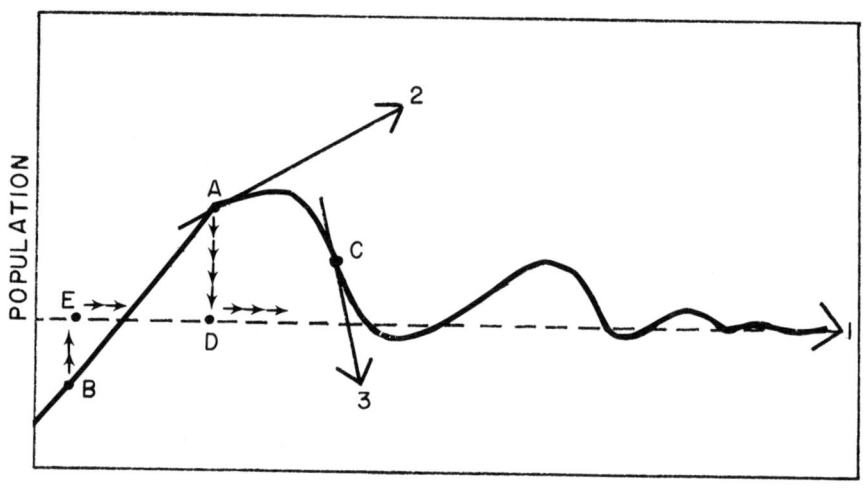

A & C--Overcapitalization   B--Undercapitalization
D & E--Points on natural growth rate
Arrows (1) Natural growth rate as described by intrinsic rate
       of natural increase; (2) Investment policy leading to
       massive overcapitalization; (3) Investment policy leading to massive undercapitalization

Figure 4.3 suggests the answer. The burden of implementation falls on the guardians of the public interest, the state authorities, and in the specific case at hand, they are the Board of Governors of the State System of Higher Education in North Carolina. The Board of Governors must ensure that above all else, there is an efficient accumulation of quality labor in the state. If the system is undercapitalized as in point B in figure 4.3 or overcapitalized as in point A, they must move the system quickly and directly to the nearest point on the natural growth rate time path such as represented by points D and E and then, they should hold firm to that time path. Such a maneuver ensures maximum efficiency in the long run (Kemeny,

Morganstern, and Thompson 1956), and forms a core for a stable, practical plan.

Population Fluctuation: Educational Supply and Demand

Next, we turn our attention to the interim problems of population fluctuation in the form of excess demand and excess supply of educational services. There is need for a responsive buffer to tide the system over in times of famine and of glut. Private enterprise is the key. Private enterprise is most noted for its quick reaction, and there exists a substantial private sector which can be used. All the state need do is provide the proper incentives in the form, perhaps, of subsidies to induce the private sector to take up the slack in time of need. It is certainly less expensive from the state's point of view to provide small, temporary subsidies to the private sector, than to embark on crash programs of capital accumulation destined to become redundant almost as soon as they are completed. However, this policy implies that the state system needs the private sector for at least the next 75 years. Moreover, present policies which are rapidly driving the private sector out of business are ill advised and should be modified. In short, once the state unilaterally adopts a reasonable core plan, the state can effectively use the private sector for complete fulfillment of social objectives.

The above buffer plan works well in times when expansion is necessary, but how does it fare in times of falling enrollments? There will be periods of excess capacity, and in these times, new uses for education must be found quickly. Certainly these periods provide perfect opportunity to exploit the consumption services rather than investment goals. On the other hand, the private sector's prime concern is to market consumable items. Again the private sector can be used to provide a needed service. Instead of wasting the taxpayer's dollars in reconverting social overhead capital to immediate consumption, an inexpensive nudge to the private sector should suffice. Moreover, the private sector is better equipped to make such a rapid response than is the cumbersome state machinery. All that is required is that the state exercise a discipline in keeping within its own proper realm of concern. In short, the plan can work in both directions.

Competing Systems

The problem of competing systems can be reduced to a minimum if the state system can exercise restraint and leadership. If the state can exercise restraint, the private sector can survive.

If the state can exercise leadership, the private sector can follow. If the state can provide proper incentives, the private sector can respond.

In sum, the approach of the stationary population presents a roller-coaster ride of challenges to higher education and I hope some day to be able to describe the situation of higher education proudly in the present tense instead of wistfully in the subjunctive.

REFERENCES

Evans, V. Jeffrey (1972) "Demand for College Professors in the State System of Higher Education of North Carolina." Ph.D. dissertation, Duke University.

Kemeny, John G.; Morganstern, Oskar; and Thompson, Gerald L. (1956) "A Generalization of the von Neumann Model of an Expanding Economy." *Econometrica* 24:115-35.

Keyfitz, Nathan (1968) *Introduction to the Mathematics of Population*. Reading, Mass.: Addison-Wesley.

Solow, Robert M. (1956) "A Contribution to the Theory of Economic Growth." *Quarterly Journal of Economics* 70:65-94.

Taylor, T. Allan, ed. (1972) *The College Blue Book*. 14th ed. New York: CCM Information Corp.

5

Speculation on Labor Mobility in a Stationary Population

HARVEY L. BROWNING

Doubtless stimulated by the striking decline in the birth rate in the U.S.A., a good deal of attention recently has been devoted to the prospect of a stationary population, how long it will take to achieve such a condition, and the socioeconomic changes that may be expected to accompany it.[1] I want to address the problem of how the condition of a stationary population will affect labor mobility in this country, examining both the amount of mobility and the forms it may assume. This topic generally is identified as social mobility. Actually, in most cases the empirical determination of social mobility is limited to occupational mobility, but in this instance I believe a single dimension of work status is too restrictive, hence the preference for the term *labor mobility*.[2] I will also concentrate my attention on intragenerational mobility--what happens to individuals in the course of their work histories--rather than intergenerational mobility, generally taken as the father-son comparison of occupational position.

There is yet another distinction that should be made clear before beginning the discussion. I want to consider only the conditions of labor mobility in a stationary population and not the features of the transition period leading to it. This is certain to be a rather lengthy interval for, as we shall later note, it is not the cessation of growth in itself that marks the stationary population, it is also a particular age structure, and this will take time to work itself out. For convenience and the greater likelihood the United States will be in or close to such a state, I assume that the conditions appropriate for a stationary population will be present by 2050, some 75 years from now, a time span adequate to permit considerable change in the country's socioeconomic structure.

Most of the work in demography has been centered on the transition period to a stationary population and the questions related to how the transformation can take place. Ansley Coale (1972) has reviewed the "alternative paths" to a stationary population, Thomas Frejka (1973) has a book out entitled, *The Future of Population Growth: Alternative Paths to Equilibrium*, and Norman Ryder (1972) stoked up his "projection engine" to produce no less than 3,125 forecasts of the U.S. population.

While the technical problems inherent in getting from here to there are intriguing in their own right and certainly have merited the attention they have received, there has been much less work devoted to the many social and economic adjustments that will be necessary during the transition period. They pose a rather different set of problems than those that can be addressed to a stationary population.

At present some of the most important and problematic developments in labor absorption and mobility involve females and minorities. The recent very impressive rise in the participation rates of women may or may not continue, although the "fertility regime" appropriate for transition to a stationary population (low reproductive rates) would imply relatively high female participation rates. But apart from how many are to be employed, the kinds of jobs that females and minorities get has an obvious bearing on labor mobility during the transition period. One forecast maintains that as it becomes increasingly difficult to absorb more people into stable and remunerative jobs, Anglo males will react strongly against women and minorities if they believe their own prospects for employment are threatened, and this will restrict the opportunities for the latter two groups. These aspects are worthy of extended consideration, but they cannot be taken up here. I will assume that in the 75 years or so of the transition period these problems will be resolved in some fashion, for better or for worse. This assumption may not be warranted, but it serves as my justification for ignoring female and minority problems in the subsequent discussion.[3]

U.S.A.--2050

So climb into my time machine and be transported to the U.S.A. *circa* 2050. I will consider it as a closed population, with all entries accounted for by births and all departures by deaths. This is not a realistic assumption, for there is certain to be some international migration. But who can know what will be the volume of entries and exits 75 years from now, for this will depend on a political resolution of government immigration policies. Probably they will be more rather than less restrictive than at present, but illegal entries--particularly from Mexico, a country that then doubtless will be in excess of 200 million--may be larger.

Demographic Considerations

In discussing a stationary population, of paramount importance, demographically, is the age composition. As Coale (1972:592) notes, ". . . the number of persons at any given age (say age 30) does not change from year to year, because 30-year-olds are the survivors (with the same proportion surviving) of the same number of births. Hence, the stationary population is not only constant in size, but also in age composition." The shape of the distribution is changed from the steeply sloped pyramidal form of today to the cylindrical form of a stationary population, as may be appreciated by a glance at table 5.1, based on Coale estimates for 2050. By the age category 60-64, a time when the work career of most persons is nearing an end, there is only a 12.5 percent loss in numbers from that in the 0-4 category. In other words, of those born in a stationary population, seven of every eight persons can expect to live through the working years.

The implications for vertical mobility in the shift from a pyramidal to a cylindrical form, and a cylinder that does not change its size, has intrigued a number of people. Nathan Keyfitz (1973) recently has examined the matter. The thrust of his argument is expressed in his first two sentences: "An increasing population facilitates individual mobility. One of the consequences of moving toward the inevitable stationary population is that mobility will become more difficult" (1973:335). The remainder of his article is devoted to a mathematical demonstration of "the pure effect of population on promotion, in abstraction from all other circumstances."

The procedure of Keyfitz, as indicated in table 5.2, is to establish five populations, whose growth rate varies from 0 to 4 percent per annum, and then to calculate the age of passing certain "gateways," which are determined by the ratio of those above to those below the individual. These arbitrary ratios vary from 3:1 to 1:5, that is, in the first instance there are three above the individual and one below, and in the second instance one above and five below.

The individual passes through all gateways at an earlier age in the population growing at 4 percent per annum. There is, however, some variation in the range between 0 and 4 percent per annum growth for particular gateways. It goes from a low of 4.8 years for K = 3 to a high of 8.1 for K = 1.0 and then declines to 6.2 for K = 0.2

Table 5.1. Projected Female Population by Age with Constant Annual Number of Births

Age Category	Numbers (in 000's)
0-4	8,890
5-9	8,875
10-14	8,863
15-19	8,850
20-24	8,823
25-29	8,809
30-34	8,768
35-39	8,728
40-44	8,660
45-49	8,565
50-54	8,403
55-59	8,159
60-64	7,779
65-69	7,156
70-74	6,193
75-79	4,811
80-84	3,388
85+	2,967

SOURCE: Coale (1972: table 1).

The reason why mobility is fostered by rapid growth does not depend on any change in the structure, it requires only that it be enlarged. Assume that there are 5,000 high status positions at the peak of a hierarchical structure. Assume too that it takes 30 years to reach that level. If it also takes 30 years for the population to double, then the individual may expect 10,000 high status positions by the time he arrives at the top level because the number of positions will have doubled at all levels.

The Keyfitz model is one of promotion upward through a hierarchical structure, even though he is in the main dealing with populations. At one point he does introduce organizations and mentions that the growth rate for particular organizations can vary much more--he suggests a range of -10 to +10 percent per annum--than for general populations. The fact that mobility in its vertical dimension takes place, in the great majority of cases, within particular organizational structures obviously weakens the value of any discussion of mobility within populations as a whole, a vexing matter that we shall return to at a later point.

Table 5.2. Age of Passing Successive Mobility Gateways by Per Annum Population Growth Rates

	r=0.00	r=0.01	r=0.02	r=0.03	r=0.04
k=3	30.31	28.75	27.45	26.38	25.51
k=2.8	30.85	29.24	27.88	26.76	25.84
k=2.6	31.46	29.78	28.36	27.18	26.21
k=2.4	32.15	30.40	28.91	27.66	26.63
k=2.2	32.92	31.09	29.53	28.21	27.12
k=2.0	33.79	31.89	30.24	28.84	27.68
k=1.8	34.79	32.81	31.07	29.58	28.34
k=1.6	35.95	33.88	32.04	30.46	29.12
k=1.4	37.31	35.15	33.21	31.51	30.06
k=1.2	38.92	36.68	34.62	32.80	31.23
k=1.0	40.86	38.55	36.39	34.43	32.71
k=0.8	43.26	40.91	38.64	36.54	34.66
k=0.6	46.31	43.97	41.64	39.41	37.35
k=0.4	50.32	48.14	45.86	43.56	41.33
k=0.2	55.93	54.27	52.36	50.27	48.08

SOURCE: Taken from Keyfitz (1973: table 2). Based on the 1968 life table for U.S. males.

Alfred Sauvy (1969) has stated the thesis that status mobility will be lower in a stationary population. It is understandable that the French, more than any other people, have been obsessed with the prospect of a stationary and even a declining population, for in the 1930s the latter possibility seemed very likely. Sauvy concludes, ". . . population growth makes the structure of occupations adaptable and progress more beneficial. The quicker the progress the sharper the demographic growth required" (1969:194). In his term, any "distortion" in the occupational pattern will take longer to correct in a stationary rather than a growing population, because youths are more flexible to adapt.

This point that structural change in the labor force is more readily accomplished in a growing population also is held by Ryder who states:

> Changes in the aggregate demand for labor which require changes in the role-specific distribution of training of the existing labor force can be accommodated either by what I term *mutation* (the changes in occupation made by particular individuals during their active lives, perhaps through retraining) and by *metabolism* (the movement into it by new members and out of it by old members). Industrial shifts in the U.S. have been accomplished mainly through metabolism. . . (1973:54-55).

Thus, the three demographers cited here agree that population growth makes for more mobility, although the emphasis is different. Keyfitz sees the greater mobility as a consequence of the expansion not the alteration of the employment structure, while Ryder and Sauvy argue that structural alteration is facilitated by growth because successive entry cohorts, each larger than the last, will have a relatively greater impact upon the total structure than is the case in a stationary population, where entry cohorts differ very little in size.

Sociological Considerations

If it is accepted that mobility is fostered in a growing population, we must recognize that there are many unanswered questions that cannot be properly addressed only by a demographic perspective. It is, therefore, necessary to introduce some sociological considerations bearing on the vertical mobility of individuals.

Sociologists have made the distinction between two kinds of mobility: *exchange* (sometimes called individual or pure) and *structural* (group).[4] Exchange mobility is the vertical movement of individuals from one hierarchically located position to another. As such, it does not require any change in the number or kind of positions themselves, but it does assume that as some persons move up others move down. Many of the great literary treatments of mobility, such as Stendhal's *The Red and the Black* or Mann's *Buddenbrooks*, follow the ascending and descending fortunes of individuals or families within the framework of exchange mobility. Structural mobility refers to some fundamental alteration in the positions themselves that will materially affect the mobility chances of large numbers of persons. The source of structural change may be an abrupt event such as a revolution or long-term secular changes such as industrialization and urbanization.

It should be apparent that the distinction between exchange and structural mobility is an analytical one, for they are rarely if ever mutually exclusive. Conceivably, it is possible to have exchange mobility with no structural mobility, but it is quite rare to have an absence of those conditions that foster structural mobility.

But what can be said about the conditions affecting structural mobility in the United States of 2050 and its stationary population? This is a very difficult question to confront, not only because many unforseeable changes may take place before 2050, but also because there is no consensus and therefore inadequate guidelines as to what structural factors are significant in bringing about labor mobility, especially vertical mobility. I propose only to briefly consider some of the long-term structural trends in American society that seem to me to have an impact on labor mobility, but no attempt is made to estimate their relative importance. Indicators of change in five areas will be presented: (1) population distribution; (2) transformation of the labor force; (3) bureaucratization; (4) education; and (5) parentage. Each of the indicators is given for 1900 and for 1970 to show the changes during these seventy years, and an estimate for 2050 is provided. This last is not intended as a forecast of what is likely to occur but rather, given the levels of 1970, what is reasonably possible over the next 80 years, as an extrapolation of the trends from 1900 to 1970. My assumption in presenting the indicators is that they are not independent of one another, and that singly and conjointly they have an important, but not an exclusive, effect on labor mobility. See table 5.3.

One feature of table 5.3 is immediately apparent. For every one of the indicators, the change indicated for 1970-2050 is less, and in most cases, much less, than that for 1900-70. Why is this? In some cases, notably for urbanization and metropolitanization, there is a ceiling effect. With nearly three-quarters of the population living in urban places in 1970, it is literally impossible for the percentage point gain of 33 between 1900 and 1970 to be matched. For a variety of reasons, it is not likely that the degree of urbanization ever will much exceed the figure of 85 percent. For example, even if agriculture and other primary activities could be fully automated, the growing conversion of nonurban land for urban uses--second home, recreational activities, et cetera--would guarantee that the population never would closely approximate 100 percent. Some of the other indicators, particularly those dealing with bureaucratization and education, are a good deal less constrained in their possible change and therefore are much more problematic.

Table 5.3. Indicators of Structural Change--United States, 1900-2050

Indicators	1900	1970	2050E
Population Distribution			
1. Percent urban	40	73	85
2. Percent metropolitan	32	69	80
Labor Force			
3. Percent in agriculture	37	4	3
4. Percent white-collar	18	50	62
Bureaucratization			
5. Percent self-employed	34	10	8
6. Percent employed in 185 largest manufacturing firms	8	30	35
7. Percent of labor force who are government employed	3	14	19
Education			
8. Implied mean duration of schooling in years	8	14	16
Parentage			
9. Percent foreign born	15	5	3

SOURCE: Indicators 1-5, 7, and 9, from U.S. decennial census reports; 6, Lebergott (1968: table 9); 8, B. Duncan (1968: table 5).

My contention is that the five areas and their indicators covered in table 5.3 all moved between 1900 and 1970 in ways that fostered labor mobility, and on a *net* basis all stimulated upward occupational mobility. The movement off the farms and out of rural areas as part of the great urbanization process of the twentieth century made it possible for millions to experience upward occupational mobility, in addition to the change of communities and work places. Urbanization made it more convenient to provide an increasing proportion of the population with higher levels of education than could be done in a dispersed rural population. The rise in white-collar employment is linked to the foregoing changes. It is perhaps too heterogeneous a category, but within it the less ambiguous professional and technical sector rose from 4 percent of the total labor force in 1900 to 16 percent in 1970.

The area of bureaucratization returns us to the problem first introduced when discussing Keyfitz: the organizational context of mobility, particularly vertical mobility. All other things being equal, within the cylinder form of the stationary age structure upward mobility would be more difficult. But of course all other things are not equal, one of them being the degree and forms of bureaucratization.

Individuals experience mobility within concrete organizations, as a rule, not within the populations as a whole, so within the cylindrical container of the stationary population there can be all sorts of geometrical forms corresponding to the concrete organizations through which people move in and out of and up or down within. Most important, the degree and kind of bureaucratization can have an effect independent of the educational and labor force characteristics of the population. While no one would dispute the increase in bureaucratization in this century, there are a number of problems in its conceptualization and especially in its measurement. Increasing bureaucratization does not mean that everyone works in huge factories or gigantic offices. The postmaster in a small town may have only an assistant, and perhaps not even that, but he is located within the single largest organization within the country, and it is this larger structure that determines his conditions of employment and prospects for advancement.

All the figures presented in table 5.3 for the 1970-2050 period extend the trends observed in the 1900-70 period, although at much slower rates. It is by no means improbable that a number of the indicators may be halted and even reversed in the years ahead, although I doubt that there ever will be a marked reversal. Consider the case of education. I have increased the mean years of schooling to 16, only about two years more than at present. But the events of the last several years have raised doubts about the capacity of the employment structure to absorb in jobs appropriate to their training the large number of college trained individuals. Similarly, the increase in the proportion of the labor force in white-collar occupations to 62 percent by 2050 may not actually take place. A few years ago there was a good deal of counter-culture talk about the movement back to the land to engage in subsistence farming and handicraft work, but this seems to be subsiding and it is unlikely that the numbers of people involved would be very great. Probably more important would be changes induced by such rather unforeseen events as the energy crisis. As my colleague Parker Frisbie has pointed out to me, a shift from petroleum to coal as the major source of the country's energy would require a very substantial increase in the employment of miners and related occupations.* These jobs will be unmistakedly blue collar (even though the monetary rewards may exceed those of many white collar occupations) and if this combines with other trends the shift to white-collar employment may be very much slowed down.

But my intention, if I may repeat it, is not to make a forecast of the employment structure in 2050, but to demonstrate that the trends observable during the first seven decades of the twentieth century are unlikely to have nearly the same force during the next eight decades or so. My conclusion, therefore, is that many, if by no means all, of the structural trends that have fostered labor mobility, especially upward mobility in the U.S.A., will have lost much of their force by 2050. The possibility that some of the trends that I have extended to that period may not actually carry through serves to strengthen rather than weaken my argument. This conclusion, of course, is in addition to the arguments of demographers already reviewed that a stationary population would be more unfavorable for upward mobility.

WAYS OF STIMULATING LABOR MOBILITY IN A STATIONARY POPULATION

If the prior discussion is correct, at least in broad terms if not in detail, the structural conditions fostering labor mobility, especially in its vertical dimension, will be less important in the United States of 2050 than at present. Does this mean that American society will become more "rigid" and less adaptable? Put this way, the question recalls the debate that raged in the early 1950s about the "rigidification" of American society. Much of it was inconclusive because of the lack of rigor in stating the problem and the scant evidence brought to bear on it, much of it highly inferential. As O. D. Duncan (1968:679) has noted, in the succeeding period relevant data began to appear, but "the decisive rejection of the rigidification thesis was accomplished by narrowing the scope of the

---

* Parker Frisbie 1974: personal communication.

issue to the question of what had been the trend in intergenerational occupation mobility." And to some extent the rigidification thesis is now to be found in the guise of "inheritance of poverty."

Even within the context of this chapter, which concentrates on intragenerational rather than intergenerational mobility, the matter is by no means clearcut. So far, the entire discussion has been predicated on the assumption that inherently there are advantages in promoting labor mobility, including occupational mobility, in a stationary population. Lincoln Day (1972) has quite a different viewpoint. He maintains, "Whether a lower rate of social mobility is to be viewed with satisfaction or alarm is largely a matter of values. . . ." He believes that a stationary population will bring about a decline in competitiveness and in level of aspiration ". . . which--given a lower actual rate of social mobility--would be the more rational psychic response" (1972:667).

Day's appraisal is at odds with those of the demographers already cited, especially Sauvy. Is it just a case of different values? I think not. Day is concerned with the effect of mobility on the level of the individual and he is particularly concerned with those who are not successful. Sauvy, on the other hand, sees the matter from the societal perspective and the impact on collective adaptation. So the heart of the difference may not be one of values but of perspective and level of analysis. It must be stressed that on both the individual and societal level no one yet has been able to show, in any precise and empirically convincing manner, just what are the consequences of different rates and kinds of labor mobility.

My own orientation, which I will not try to justify, is that, all in all, labor mobility is preferable because it increases the flexibility within a social system. Moreover, given the trends previously identified that would serve to limit mobility, it is more challenging to review ways of stimulating mobility than to simply say that a stationary population induces a decline in social mobility and this is a good thing. And my concern with labor mobility is not limited to vertical mobility, but also geographic and horizontal job changes.

On the face of it there is no inherent reason why stationary populations can't be dynamic and capable of fostering considerable mobility. If the labor force is conceived of as a set of structured and hierarchically arranged positions, and if under the conditions of a stationary population and a "mature" socioeconomic structure the rate of change in both the number and the kind of positions is lower than at present, there still can be a good deal of mobility by shifting persons in and out of positions.

How can this be accomplished? Keyfitz (1973:348) suggests what might be termed a pseudo-solution. By the creation of more "markers of social status" through the creation of new titles and greater symbolic differentiation of positions, the amount of mobility could be increased. But Keyfitz himself is doubtful that such contrived distinctions would be accepted as real and would have the intended effect of motivating people to actively seek such positions.

Migration

Of course, labor mobility can be encouraged in its nonvertical dimensions. Both individuals and their societies may benefit from changes originating in the shift of community of residence and in changes in work-place that do not entail a change in kind of work performed.

Blau and Duncan (1967:275) in their analysis of change of residence through migration conclude that "The community in which a man is raised, just as the race or ethnic group into which he is born, defines an ascriptive base that limits his occupational chances. Migration, however, partly removes these ascribed restrictions on achievement by enabling a man to take advantage of opportunities not available in his original community." They, of course, have in mind the enhanced potential for vertical mobility, but geographic mobility in itself may enable a person to do a better job, even if remaining at the same vertical level. Kuznets (1964), in his discussion of the advantages of migration, argues that, other things being equal, the migrant will have an advantage over the native because of his greater "detachment," meaning that he is less subject to kinship and community influences and therefore presumably more able to devote his attention to his work.

Rather similar arguments to those advanced for migration can be adduced for change of work-place that does not require change in actual work duties. People may grow stale in their routine, may reach the limits of growth possible in a particular position, or may experience interpersonal difficulties that will limit their effectiveness. A change of work sites could significantly improve their performance.

Age of Entry and Exit

If a stationary population means fewer work positions are created, one way to increase mobility is to alter the age of entry and exit into the labor force. Higher education and the increasing proportion of the population that experience it has worked to delay full-time entry into the labor force. But it seems unlikely that there will be any significant increase in age of entry into the labor force by 2050. Indeed, it is possible that it may decline somewhat. There is a growing realization that prolonged schooling may have deleterious effects on young people. In recent years, a number of individuals have argued that late adolescents and young adults should not be kept in schools for long consecutive periods. They urge more exposure to the "real" world, especially for those who go on to college, through job experience interspersed with schooling. This approach, parenthetically, is stressed by socialist countries such as China and Cuba, evidently with some success.

Early exits from the labor force can have a greater impact, for age and seniority are necessarily linked. Anything that serves to remove persons from the upper levels of hierarchies should allow for greater upward mobility, although not all older persons are located in the upper levels. Early retirement can take two forms: (1) complete retirement, with full benefits at ages before 65, a route that has been pushed by a number of labor unions for ages between 55 and 65; and (2) partial retirement, representing a gradual withdrawal from the labor force.

One thing is certain. Both delayed entries and early exits from the labor force are sure to be very costly for the societies involved; certainly, there would be little justification for adopting these practices on the basis only of enhanced mobility. But from the standpoint of the individual there are also disadvantages. For example, the 20 or more years of schooling, often continuous, needed to complete the doctoral degree may "warp" the individual in ways not fully recognized. At the other end of the work cycle, early retirement may offer nothing more than the dreary prospect of a long period of enforced idleness. Even should there be only a few years increase in life expectancy between now and 2050, the retirement span could average well beyond 10 years.

Multiple Careers

A more innovative solution to the problem of fostering mobility is one of providing for multiple work careers, a way of increasing the circulation among positions, even though the number and kind of positions remains relatively unchanged. Permitting individuals to engage in two or more careers during their work lives means that after moving up through the hierarchy in one line of work (not generally to the top) a switch to a different line of work would require starting at a lower level, often necessitating going through a training or apprenticeship program. Such a switch may or may not prolong the individual's work life.

The position left vacant by a move to another kind of work either could be filled by the promotion of someone within the hierarchy, by bringing someone in from outside, or by abolishing the position and creating a new one at a lower level.[5]

Difficulties in Stimulating Mobility

Whatever the forms adopted for stimulating mobility in 2050, the difficulties in doing so should not be underestimated. In somewhat cryptic fashion Sauvy (1969:202) remarks,

> If the population reacts against its own rigidity, it may achieve sufficient mobility of labor. But since the stationary position has a stabilizing influence, there would need to be exceptional responsibility here for the population not to fall victim of laziness. A socialist society would in principle be better suited to solve this internal problem, but even here there would be considerable difficulties.

"Laziness" in this context must mean an unwillingness to seek new alternatives for the promotion of mobility. Sauvy doesn't make it clear why a socialist society would be better suited than a capitalist one. Perhaps he had in mind the distinction between a centrally planned versus noncentrally planned society and the greater power the former has to implement policy directives. In these terms, however, a fascist society could be just as effective as a socialist one.

What does seem to me to be crucial in this discussion is the point that many, if not all, of the suggestions for promoting labor mobility would be more difficult to carry out in the "free labor" system that capitalism entails. To coordinate the various kinds of mobility in such a way that maximum benefits accrue to both individuals and the society would be quite difficult to do within a capitalist system.

Take, for example, the notion of multiple careers. A major reason why this phenomenon is not common in American society is the great financial risks it generally entails. Anyone who has advanced in a particular career and who then wishes to shift to another one often is deterred from making the change because of the substantial cut in earnings necessitated in starting again near the bottom in another line of work. Since in many cases the individual is in the stage of the family life cycle when the "dependency" demands are near the maximum, the risk of venturing a change appears too great to all but a few intrepid souls.

The point is not that job shifts should never entail a cut in earnings; only that it not be so severe as to make the shift untenable. Probably some form of guaranteed annual income--not limited to the lower income strata--would be the best institutional arrangement for facilitating not only multiple careers but also most of the other forms of mobility that have been discussed here. Thus, we arrive at one of the paradoxes of the modern condition: to provide individuals with more freedom of choice we must impose more "control" at another level by some government agency. This is not easy to do, but perhaps by 2050 some of the ideological shibboleths that now encumber consideration of such arrangements will have lost their force. Some judicious combination of material and moral incentives to supplement a form of guaranteed income might be the answer, especially in accommodating the ambitious ones.

CONCLUSION

Any discussion of American society in mid-twenty-first century must be an exercise in futurology in which the method is one of ratiocination, to be judged in terms of its plausibility. Like science fiction, futurology should not be judged by its predictive power. Doubtless, in 2050 social scientists will have more important concerns than checking out the forecasts of present-day futurologists.

In any event, I believe the value of such speculative inquiry is not so much the power to peer into the future. Rather, it is helpful in appraising the current understanding of our society, for we are forced to ask questions and consider problems that otherwise might not be raised. In this instance, by trying to imagine what will be the degree and forms of labor mobility in 2050 I have been made more aware of the limitations and deficiencies of present-day approaches to the study of social mobility.

Few fields within sociology have drawn more attention and sustained interest than social mobility, a subject that has recently brought forth an unusual number of cross-national studies. Yet, when the large amount of work on social mobility is examined, the situation is not encouraging. The heart of the problem, in my opinion, lies in the unit of analysis adopted. The great preponderance of work is devoted to explaining the behavior of individuals rather than the transformation of the opportunity structures through which they pass. Raymond Boudon makes this point in his critique of the status attainment approach as exemplified by Blau and Duncan (1967). Boudon says:

. . . a number of structural explanatory variables on

which the son's status also depends (over time change in the social structure, "discrepancy" between the educational and the social structure) are excluded from the model, simply because they are not defined for individuals. Interestingly enough, this is probably why the proportion of variance of the dependent variable (son's status) explained by the independent variables (father's status, father's education, etc.) appears in Blau and Duncan (1967) as smaller than its *unexplained* proportion (1973:137).

A key consideration is the distinction between structural and exchange mobility, one central to the prior discussion but admittedly one that involves many difficulties. Often, the distinction is made along the lines suggested by Matras (1967). In the change between two periods, structural mobility is the minimum shifts of individuals needed to produce the observed changes in the distribution of individuals among categories (however defined). What is left over, the residual, is termed exchange mobility.

Harrison White, in his pathbreaking 1970 work, criticizes this procedure:

> Jobs like men have life histories; they are not only born, they die. In even the most stable system, with unchanging marginal distributions, there is a constant turnover of particular jobs. If structural mobility is to denote mobility necessitated by changing objective needs in productive activity, gross rather than net changes in jobs should be considered. That is, flows of new jobs must be kept separate and not balanced off against departures of jobs, and the changes should be measured in absolute numbers and not in percentages. It is probably useful to expand the definition to include the need for replacements to men who die and disappear. Exchange mobility should be replaced by chain mobility, the mobility described by the multiplier effect. The latter is not a residual concept; it is mobility lawfully dependent on structural mobility, using the revised and expanded definition of the latter (1970:246).

White approaches the duality of men and jobs in terms of a vacancy chain model, and he has empirically applied it to the clergy of the Episcopal church. It remains to be seen whether it is possible to consider the social system as a kind of organization, but White's approach is quite promising in its implications. Whatever the route taken, the agenda for research on labor and social mobility in the future should place more emphasis on structural sources of change and their measurement than has been true in the past.

NOTES

1. In addition to this volume, there is the recent provocative collection of articles published under the title, *The No-Growth Society* (Olson and Landsberg 1973).

2. The perspective in this chapter is that of demography and sociology. Labor mobility also can be viewed from an economic perspective, but I am not competent to deal with it. Aside from the articles by economists in *The No-Growth Society*, probably the best source is *Economic Aspects of Population Change* (Morss and Reed, eds., 1972), especially the article by Joseph J. Spengler, "Declining Population Growth: Economic Effects."

3. Most of the efforts to make projections of the labor force for some time in the future seem rather mechanical and unenlightening. For an exception, see the wide-ranging and stimulating article by Johnston (1972) that presents figures up to 2040.

4. For a good recent review of the various measures of mobility see Boudon (1973).

5. This latter option increasingly is being adopted by the central administration of many universities who suddenly find themselves in a condition of no growth. Formerly, it had been taken for granted in the event of the loss of a full professorship through retirement or resignation that the position would be filled by someone of the same rank, in order to maintain the prestige of the department at relatively the same level. Nowadays, the no-growth situation effectively has introduced a restriction of departmental autonomy, for the administration, in order to assure mobility throughout the hierarchy, has reserved the right to reduce the position to that of assistant professor.

REFERENCES

Beyle, Marie Henri [Stendahl] (1969) *The Red and the Black*. Translated and edited by Robert M. Adams. New York: Norton.

Blau, Peter and Duncan, Otis Dudley (1967) *The American Occupational Structure*. New York: Wiley.

Boudon, Raymond (1973) *Mathematical Structures of Social Mobility*. San Francisco: Jossey-Bass.

Coale, Ansley J. (1972) "Alternate Paths to a Stationary Population," in Westoff and Parke, *Demographic and Social Aspects of Population Growth*.

Day, Lincoln (1972) "The Social Consequences of a Zero Population Growth Rate in the United States," in Westoff and Parke, *Demographic and Social Aspects of Population Growth*.

Duncan, Beverly (1968) "Trends in Output and Distribution of Schooling," in Sheldon and Moore, *Indicators of Social Change*.

Duncan, Otis Dudley (1968) "Social Stratification and Mobility: Problems in the Measurement of Trends," in Sheldon and Moore, *Indicators of Social Change*.

Frejka, Tomas (1973) *The Future of Population Growth: Alternative Paths to Equilibrium*. New York: Wiley.

Johnston, Denis F. (1972) "Illustrative Projections of the Labor Force of the United States to 2040," in Morss and Reed, *Economic Aspects of Population Change*.

Keyfitz, Nathan (1973) "Individual Mobility in a Stationary Population." *Population Studies* 27(2):335-52.

Kuznets, Simon (1964) Introduction to *Demographic Analyses and Interrelations*, edited by Hope T. Eldridge and Dorothy Swaine Thomas, Population Redistribution and Economic Growth, United States, 1870-1950, vol. 3. Philadelphia: The American Philosophical Society.

Lebergott, Stanley (1968) "Labor Force and Employment Trends," in Sheldon and Moore, *Indicators of Social Change*.

Mann, Thomas (1965) *Buddenbrooks*. Translated by H. T. Lowe-Porter. New York: Knopf.

Matras, Judah (1967) "Social Mobility and Social Structure: Some Insights from the Linear Model." *American Sociological Review* 32:608-14.

Morss, Elliott R. and Reed, Ritchie H., eds. (1972) *Economic Aspects of Population Change,* Commission on Population and the American Future Research Reports, vol. 2. Washington: U.S. Government Printing Office.

Olson, Mancur and Landsberg, Hans H., eds. (1973) *The No-Growth Society*. New York: Norton.

Ryder, Norman (1972) "A Demographic Optimum Projection for the United States," in Westoff and Parke, *Demographic and Social Aspects of Population Growth*.

_____ (1973) "Two Cheers for ZPG," in Olson and Landsberg, *The No-Growth Society*.

Sauvy, Alfred (1969) *General Theory of Population*. New York: Basic Books.

Sheldon, Elanor Bernert and Moore, Wilbert E., eds. (1968) *Indicators of Social Change*. New York: Russell Sage.

Spengler, Joseph J. (1972) "Declining Population Growth: Economic Effects," in Morss and Reed, *Economic Aspects of Population Change*.

Westoff, Charles F. and Parke, Robert, Jr., eds. (1972) *Demographic and Social Aspects of Population Growth,* Commission on Population Growth and the American Future Research Reports, vol. 1. Washington: U.S. Government Printing Office.

White, Harrison (1970) *Chains of Opportunity: System Models of Mobility in Organizations*. Cambridge, Mass.: Harvard University Press.

6

Stationary Populations: Pensions and the Social Security System

BOONE A. TURCHI

The prospect of zero population growth in the United States leads to numerous questions about the impact of a stationary population on the country's social and economic life. This chapter represents my initial effort to study in a comprehensive way the economic implications of a stationary population. As such, it is exploratory and tentative in nature, raising more questions than can be answered; moreover, it treats only a small part of the total question: the impact of zero population growth on the old age pension system.

In this country two systems have evolved which provide the aged with income during the years following retirement. The first system is the Old Age Survivors, Disability and Health Insurance (OASDHI) program, administered by the federal government. The second is the private pension system administered by numerous corporations, businesses, and financial institutions across the nation. Both systems are intimately connected with the nation's demographic structure since they exist to serve a distinct demographic group--the aged.

While the two systems serve the same demographic group, their respective influences on the aggregate economy are manifested through different channels. Therefore, each system will be

---

This is a slightly revised version of a paper presented at the annual meeting of the Population Association of America, 20 April 1974, in New York. I would like to thank Peter Jones, Francis Horvath, William Serow, and Peter Grandstaff for helpful comments, and Mrs. Betsy Pierce for her skillful typing.

discussed independently with respect to (1) its structure and history, (2) its impact on the aggregate economy, and (3) its response to the demographic changes wrought by the advent of zero growth.

We know very little about the second and third items on this list--research in the economics of stationary populations is still in its infancy, and, as I will argue at the conclusion of this paper, new approaches to the study of aggregate economic-demographic relationships are absolutely necessary if our understanding of these relationships is to be advanced appreciably. Specifically, I will argue that the demographic changes wrought by the advent of zero population growth are so pervasive that nothing less than a general systems analysis of their impact on the aggregate economy is warranted.

THE STATIONARY POPULATION

In the discussion that follows, it will be assumed that the United States has reached the stationary population projected by the U.S. Census Bureau and illustrated in table 6.1. For our purposes the two salient features of the ultimate stationary population pictured in table 6.1 are (1) its stable age distribution with high median age relative to the current United States population and (2) the constant size of the economically active population. The approach of the economy to the stationary population state will not be considered, nor will the overall response of the economy to zero population growth be emphasized. Finally we will abstract from the role of the United States in the world economy. It is likely that this country will reach the stationary state long before the vast majority of the world's population. The implications of this possibility for the present analysis will be ignored although they should explicitly be included in any more general analysis of the economic system's response to zero population growth.

OASDHI AND THE STATIONARY STATE

The first significant excursion of the United States into the unmapped terrain of the welfare state began in September, 1934. In one hectic year the Social Security program was conceived, planned, and enacted by Congress. The system as originally conceived was to be supported through tripartite contributions by workers, employers, and the federal government. To this day, however, the government has made no contributions to the system and it remains a compulsory social insurance system contributed to by employers and employees exclusively.

Table 6.1. Age Distribution of the Population Moving to a Stationary State Under ZPG Conditions, 1970 to Ultimate Stationary State

Category	1970	1985	2000	2025	2050	Ultimate Stationary
Population in thousands						
Ages 0-19	17,150	76,228	78,359	78,225	78,088	77,848
Ages 20-64	107,497	131,675	149,335	162,355	163,853	163,933
Ages 65 and over	20,156	25,274	28,052	42,442	46,074	46,213
Total Population	204,800	233,179	255,747	283,021	288,016	288,112
Percent of Population age 65 and over	9.8	10.8	11.0	15.0	16.0	16.0
Ratio of age 65 and over to ages 20-64	.188	.192	.188	.261	.281	.282
Percent of ratio over 1970 ratio	100	102	100	139	149	150
Median age in years	27.9	30.1	33.4	36.7	37.3	37.3

SOURCE: Rejda (1973) as computed from U.S. Bureau of the Census (1972: table 7).

As it has evolved, the OASDHI system has manifested two major goals: (1) to prevent poverty and economic dependency in old age, and (2) to help moderate the decline in living standards experienced when the earnings of a family head cease because of retirement, disability, or death (Pechman, Aaron, and Tausig 1967:5). Although conceived as a social insurance scheme, OASDHI can hardly be compared to a private insurance system. In practice the relation between contributions and benefits has often been tenuous; workers with only a few years of covered employment have been systematically retired with full benefits. Furthermore, while benefits are related to some degree with contributions, the correspondence is by no means even remotely close. Present beneficiaries under OASDHI receive benefits far in excess of those to which they would be entitled based on the taxes paid either by or for them. This situation will persist as long as Congress grants benefit increases so as to keep the real level of benefits rising at roughly the same rate as real wages.

Table 6.2 traces the growth of that part of the OASDHI program devoted exclusively to the aged. While the number of workers contributing to the system almost doubled between 1950 and 1972, the number of beneficiaries increased more than eightfold. Retirement benefits (in nominal terms) increased even more rapidly, rising by more than 43 times during the period.

By now, the Social Security system expansion is virtually complete. In 1972, approximately 91 percent of all elderly persons were either receiving benefits or were eligible to do so when they or their spouses retired (Brown 1972:25). OASDHI's impact on the aggregate economy in the future will, therefore, depend on the manner in which contributions are collected, and on the real growth of benefits per capita.

The Macroeconomic Impact of OASDHI

The system which finances OASDHI is familiar to most of us--contributions to the system are collected via a flat rate payroll tax levied on both employees and employers. The flat rate is collected on each dollar of wage earnings up to a legally specified maximum. In 1974, the Social Security tax of 5.85 percent for both employee and employer on the first $13,200 of taxable wages would lead to a maximum annual contribution of $772.20. Self-employed persons contribute to the payroll tax at a higher rate of 7.9 percent on the first $13,200 of taxable wages.

Although originally set up to operate with a sizable reserve fund in the manner of a private pension trust, OASDHI operates basically on a pay-as-you go basis. Had the system evolved as

Table 6.2. OASDHI Retirement Benefits to Retired Workers, 1950-72

Category	1950	1955	1960	1965	1969	1970	1971	1972
Benefits paid (millions)*	$557	3,253	7,053	10,984	15,383	18,435	21,889	24,233
Average monthly benefit in 1972 dollars	74.54	98.01	105.55	111.98	113.21	126.23	136.68	161.97
Number of beneficiaries at end of year (,000's)	1,771	4,474	8,061	11,101	12,822	13,349	13,927	14,455
Number of workers with taxable earnings (millions)	48	65	73	81	89	93	94	94
Old-age and survivors trust fund ($ billions)		21.6	20.3	18.2	30.1	32.4	33.8	35.3

*Dollar amounts in current prices unless otherwise noted.

SOURCE: U.S. Bureau of the Census (1973:293).

Congress had originally intended, the Social Security trust fund would have quickly accumulated a reserve of $47 billion, which would have exceeded the entire federal debt of that period. Instead, the trust fund developed into a cushion which has served mainly to offset actuarial miscalculations and to meet unforeseen contingencies. Table 6.2 shows that the trust fund has grown relatively little over the past couple of decades--indeed, the value of the trust fund in real terms grew by only 20 percent between 1955 and 1972. Thus, today the OASDHI trust fund represents only about one year's obligations for the system.

The Social Security system is nothing more than a massive transfer of current real resources from the working population to the aged. Aside from the macroeconomic impact of this redistribution, the influence of OASDHI on the economic system is designed to be minimal. Trust funds are invested in specially designed government bonds producing yields equivalent to that achieved on medium term (4- to 7-year) government issues, and their fiscal impact would appear to be nearly neutral. Indeed, as Henry Aaron has argued (1966) a pay-as-you-go system is appropriate in an economy experiencing both economic and demographic growth. As we shall observe shortly, however, the system may prove to be less than optimal in the absence of demographic change.

Considerable debate has occurred over the question of the Social Security system's progressivity (Brittain 1971; Feldstein 1972; Campbell 1969; Rejda 1970). By itself the payroll tax is clearly regressive with upper income wage earners paying a considerably lower average rate; moreover, payroll taxes have been rising at an exceedingly rapid rate in recent years while income taxes have remained constant and the burden of the tax on middle income groups cannot be denied. For example, an individual earning at least $13,200 in 1974 will pay more than double the Social Security tax he paid in 1970, and over 65 percent more than he paid in 1972.

Proponents of the present system argue, however, that the OASDHI program must be judged in its entirety. The progressive nature of the benefit structure is argued to more than offset any regressivity embodied in the payroll tax. Retirement benefits, while rising with preretirement wage levels, increase less than proportionally. Under the 1971 benefit structure, retirees whose preretirement average monthly income put them in the lowest income group could expect to receive over 92 percent of that income in the form of Social Security benefits, while retirees in the highest bracket would receive 40 percent or less (Brown 1972:168).

Nevertheless, from a macroeconomic standpoint, the salient feature of the OASDHI system is that it is a transfer from young to old, from one demographic group to a very distinct alternate group. Given that the payroll tax is indeed burdensome, and given that it will become more burdensome with the advent of zero population growth, the macroeconomic implications of this intergenerational transfer cannot be overlooked.

In theory the transfer should stimulate consumption spending and depress aggregate saving. According to the life-cycle hypotheses of aggregate consumption (Ando and Modigliani 1963), household saving reaches a maximum during the head's fifth decade. As a household approaches the late sixties, it becomes, on the average, a net dissaver. Therefore, we expect that the income transfer generated by the Social Security system will act to depress aggregate personal saving by transferring income from the saving population to the demographic group which includes a high proportion of dissavers.

The empirical evidence on the point is virtually nonexistent--indeed, the only study with which I am familiar suggests that the opposite argument is correct. Using aggregate time series data (quarterly) for the period 1953 to 1969, Lester Taylor (1971) finds that in the very short run, at least, each dollar of payroll tax reduces personal saving by two dollars and that each dollar of transfers received is converted to only 15 cents consumption and 85 cents saving. These findings relate, of course, to extremely short-run data and the behavior which they describe may not (if it exists) carry over to longer-run behavior.

More plausible is the effect implied by the life-cycle hypothesis of aggregate saving: the transfer of income from the working population to the retired population will serve to reduce aggregate saving. This will occur, other things being equal, because (1) the disposable income of the working population will be reduced and (2) because the incentive to save for retirement is inhibited by the existence of the OASDHI program. However, without considerably more research into the impact of the program on private saving, our understanding of the macroeconomic effects of the system is likely to remain exceedingly underdeveloped.

Another economically important feature of the Social Security system is the impact it has on the supply of manpower in the economy. Although age 65 was originally chosen as the statutory minimum for retirement under OASDHI mainly in response to prevailing industry practice, it has subsequently become the guiding standard for the private system. Changes in the OASDHI statutory minimum would affect both the quantity of manpower available and the cost of the Social Security system. A decline in the size of the labor force brought about by a reduction in the statutory retirement age might exacerbate the labor shortages in the zero population growth economy which have been predicted by Professor Spengler (1972). Thus, the Social Security system may, operating through the labor market, have an effect on price and wage levels if retirement rules are liberalized to any degree. Moreover, if the economic system were to encounter chronic recession it might be expected that a political battle would arise over the minimum retirement age. Employers and younger employees might attempt to use a lower retirement age as a means to accelerate the displacement of older workers, using as justification the availability of compensation under OASDHI.

Zero Population Growth, Social Security, and the Economy

It has been suggested that OASDHI affects the economy (1) by transferring income from high savers to low savers, (2) by reducing the incentive of younger workers to save for retirement, and (3) by affecting the supply of manpower in the older age groups. In this section we will speculate on the impact that the advent of a stationary population will have both on the Social Security itself and on the aggregate economy.

George Rejda (1973) has made some calculations which conveniently illustrate the impact that zero population growth might have on the OASDHI program. He notes that the major effect of the change to a stationary population will be the shift in the age structure (table 6.1). In 1970, 9.8 percent of the population was age 65 or older; by the year 2050, if current age specific fertility rates are maintained, the age structure of the population will be essentially stable at the zero growth level and the proportion of the population aged 65 plus will have increased to 16 percent. Perhaps more significant from our point of view is the fact that the ratio of the aged population to economically active population will have risen from 0.188 to 0.281, an increase of 49 percent. Moreover, if current trends toward early retirement with reduced benefits continue or are ratified through the reduction of the legal minimum retirement age, the ratio of aged to active could rise to 0.420--an implied rise of 123 percent in the old age dependency burden.

Rejda proceeds to ask what the necessary increase in real income per capita would have to be to support this relatively large group of aged individuals: (1) if there were no increase in real OASDHI benefits, or (2) if benefits were allowed to rise. The welfare criterion that Rejda uses in both cases is that the real burden on the active population should not rise. Real per capita OASDHI benefits for aged persons in a given year, t can be expressed as:

$$B(t) = \frac{P(t) \cdot r(t) \cdot (1 - c)}{R(t)},$$

where P(t) equals real per capita personal income, r(t) equals the percent of real P(t) spent on OASDHI benefits for the aged, R(t) is the ratio of aged to active workers, and c is the proportion of total benefit payments needed to administer the system. Then, if the real burden is to remain constant, r(t) will remain unchanged over time and real benefits per capita will remain unchanged over time if and only if the ratio P(t)/R(t) remains constant (neglecting, of course, changes in administrative expenses). Consequently, if the old age dependency ratio rises by 50 percent, so must real per capita personal income. This implies an average annual growth rate of approximately one-half percent in real per capita income between 1970 and 2050.

However, the required growth rate in per capita income is larger if the trend to early retirement continues. Suppose workers aged 60 and over are retired by 2050--then, given a rise of 123 percent in the old age dependency burden, real income per capita would have to rise at the compound rate of 1.01 percent per annum to keep real benefits and real tax burden constant.

Given the recent history of Social Security benefit increases, however, it is unlikely the real benefits will remain constant over time. Benefits will rise because one of the goals of the OASDHI program is to mitigate the decline in real income experienced by newly retired workers; moreover, benefits may rise because the political power of the elderly group increases in proportion to its relative size in the population. In any case, in order to produce an annual compound increase in B(t) of g percent while keeping the real burden constant, an annual growth rate in real income per capita of (1.01 + g) percent is needed. Therefore, to increase real benefits per capita by one percent per year, a growth rate of 2.01 percent in personal income is required.

Reference to table 6.2 will confirm that during the period 1950 to 1972, real average monthly benefits grew at the annual rate of 3.52 percent, which would require a growth rate of 4.53 percent in personal income to be sustained in the stationary state. During that same period, real personal income grew at 2.67 percent per year, a rate which led to an increasing intergenerational transfer of income. Thus, to maintain anything like recent rates of growth in real benefits will require the assumption of a considerable extra burden by the working age population. Moreover, just to avoid increasing the real burden on the working age population requires absolutely that real income grow. However, it is precisely the prospects for real income growth which are called into question by the advent of zero population growth (Keynes 1937; Hansen 1939; Heiser 1973).

Thus, the advent of zero population growth will serve to reinforce some tendencies of the Social Security system as it now exists. The transfer of income from savers to relative dissavers will be accentuated by the aging of the population; the relative burden on younger workers in the economy will increase, especially if the retirement age declines as now appears to be the trend; economic growth would appear to be essential if the past growth of real economic benefits under OASDHI is to be sustained. Finally, the impact of the system on the supply of labor may have an important impact on the relative scarcity of labor and the resulting aggregate increases in wages and prices. As the relative burden on the working age population grows, intergenerational antagonisms may increase leading perhaps to pressure from both the young and the aged for relief. If aggregate personal savings do decline, the economy's capacity to support an older population through the Social Security system would be reduced perhaps necessitating a larger role for government in the economic system.

PRIVATE PENSIONS AND THE STATIONARY STATE

The other major institutional arrangement which has evolved to deal with the economic problems of aging in the United States is the private pension system. Originally begun as a means of providing relief for superannuated employees, the role of the pension scheme has developed into a major element in personnel administration. The major functions of the current pension system in the United States are (1) to operate as a device for the orderly displacement of older workers while maintaining employee morale, and (2) to attract labor to a given firm in a competitive market for qualified personnel.

As is evident from table 6.3, pension funds have undergone tremendous growth since the end of World War II. Funded claims on pension funds have increased from $24 billion in 1950 to $268 billion by 1971, an increase of 1,117 percent in nominal terms. This annual growth rate of 11.5 percent compares favorably with the 7.6 percent annual growth of financial assets in general and makes pension funds the second fastest growing institution in the nation, surpassed only by the growth of open-end investment companies. At present, pension fund reserves constitute something over 12 percent of all financial assets and, if unfunded liabilities to employees are included, they probably total close to $1 trillion. Pension saving flows have increased from $1.6 billion in 1946 to something over $20 billion annually in 1971.

Pension saving now accounts for something between one-third and two-fifths of all personal saving in the economy (table 6.4). Thus, both in terms of aggregate size and rate of growth, pension funds represent a major element of the financial system of the United States, and as such deserve study in their own right.

Table 6.3. Pension Fund Assets and Total Financial Assets Held by Households, 1950-71

	Billions of current dollars						
Category	1950	1955	1960	1965	1969	1970	1971
Total pension fund assets*	24.0	50.4	90.7	152.7	215.0	233.6	268.1
Total financial assets	442.7	700.7	957.1	1469.6	1840.3	1889.3	2170.4
Pension fund reserves as a percent of total financial assets	5.4	7.2	9.5	10.4	11.7	12.4	12.4

*Includes only funded pension fund assets held by households.

SOURCE: U.S. Bureau of the Census (1973:441)

Pension Funds and the Aggregate Economy

Since pension funds are an element in the financial system rather than the market for real goods and services, their impact on the long-range growth of the economy has not been as extensively studied as would have been desirable. In fact, scholarly research has lagged far behind in the integration of real and monetary economics in the analysis of medium- and long-term economic growth. The pension system exists in the monetary sector of the economy and its effect upon long-term economic growth cannot be analyzed in the context of traditional neoclassical models of growth. Moreover, the demographic transition to a stationary population may have important aggregate consequences for the economy which operate through the pension system or through other financial institutions; however, without a holistic approach to the impact of demographic change on the economy it may be impossible to make a meaningful assessment of future prospects.

Table 6.4. Net Investment by Households, Personal Trusts, and Nonprofit Organizations

	Billions of current dollars							
	1946	1950	1955	1960	1965	1969	1970	1971
Pension fund reserves	1.6	3.0	5.4	8.1	12.3	15.8	19.5	20.2
Personal savings NIA basis	15.9	14.4	17.6	20.1	28.4	37.9	54.1	60.5
Pension fund reserves as a percent of personal savings	10.1	20.8	30.7	40.3	43.0	41.0	36.0	33.0

SOURCE: Blackburn (1967:8); Board of Governors FRS (1972: A73.3).

In an economy characterized by a growing population, actuarily funded pension programs will represent a net addition to personal saving in the absence of substitution. A number of economists have attempted to test the hypothesis that the net impact of pensions is to promote saving. Perhaps the best known study is that of Cagan (1965) who used a survey of Consumers Union members generated in 1958 and 1959. Cagan's preliminary hypothesis was that pension saving is a good substitute for other forms of saving and that coverage under a plan should signal reductions in other forms of saving. He found just the opposite: ". . . when households come under a pension plan offsetting reductions in other saving do not occur. The net addition to aggregate personal saving apparently equals the full amount of employee's and employer's contribution" (1965:82). The average net addition to other forms of saving was in the range of one-half to 1 percent of income. Moreover, respondents with *vested* pension rights in any degree were found to save an additional 1.5 percent in other types of nonpension saving. As long as the employee's pension contributions amounted to less than 3 to 4 percent of his pay, Cagan found that pension saving and nonpension saving were complements, not substitutes. Thus the aggregate impact of pension plans on saving would appear to be positive in a growing economy.

Cagan's findings are supported to a varying degree in studies by

Katona (1965) and Schoeplein (1970). Katona used a national probability sample of American households and found that the presence of a pension plan was positively associated with discretionary (that is, noncontractual) saving. Using data from individual Canadian income tax returns, Schoeplein found that among upper income households, contributions to pension plans were positively associated with other forms of contractual *retirement* savings. However, among lower income households pension contributions appeared to substitute for other forms of retirement saving. One wonders whether the special nature of Cagan's sample precluded his discovery of the same sort of interaction effect operating among American households. Another study using aggregate National Income and Product Account data (Apilado 1972) appears to contradict the findings of Cagan and Katona. In it, aggregate personal savings appear to be negatively related to pension fund contributions; however, the statistical problems confronting Apilado's article are so severe that the validity of its results can be taken only with extreme skepticism.

Proceeding under the assumption that the direct and indirect effects of pension plans are to increase aggregate saving, we may inquire as to their impact on the macroeconomy. It would appear that the growth of pension plans has served to offset the negative impact on savings attributed to the OASDHI system; indeed, aggregate savings might be higher given the presence of these two programs than in their absence. At least one commentator (Blackburn 1967) has suggested that the pension system results in a level of saving which, in the long run, will be too large for the economy to absorb, and this will in turn result in aggregate demand insufficient to avoid chronic unemployment. In this scenario, the private saving induced by the pension system would require public dissaving and an increasing role for the federal government in order to maintain full employment of resources. Until the basic econometric estimates have been made, however, this will remain an unsupported hypothesis. Nevertheless it does point to a major area of interest for research: the role of the federal government in the social and economic system as a consequence of zero population growth.

Beneficiaries must rely on accumulated financial claims which will be transformed to direct claims on current goods and services at the time of retirement. Often these financial claims are denominated in fixed nominal amounts and, as a result, stable prices are essential if the real income of retirees is not to be eroded significantly. In order to support the retired population, the economically active population must acquiesce in the sharing of current resources. If the claim of the retired population on current goods and services seems burdensome, the younger population may be tempted to lighten the burden through inflation (Murray 1968). Of course, if real incomes are generally rising, the demands of the older population will seem less oppressive, even in the face of a major shift in the age structure of the population. Again, the impact of demographic change on the pension system and economy is shown to depend on the total response of the aggregate system to demographic change, not just the response operating through the financial system. The pension system is just one element of a complex economy that contains many interdependent parts, and the transition to zero population growth will affect all parts of this general system.

For example, pension funds are demonstrating an increasing interest in investing in the mortgage market. This market is developing to the point that the management of a mortgage portfolio is almost as convenient as the management of a bond portfolio. This suggests that pension funds will eventually become major participants in housing finance. Yet, at the same time, the advent of a stationary population will have a profound impact on the aggregate demand for housing. If zero population growth reduces the supply of funds that the pension system is able to place in the mortgage market while it simultaneously reduces the aggregate demand for housing, a major component of aggregate demand will be severely affected from two different directions, but from the same ultimate source. A partial analysis that focuses strictly on the financial sector or on the demand side of the housing market will produce a distorted and incorrect view of the total impact of demographic change.

Zero Population Growth, Pensions, and the Economy

The change in the quantity of pension funds allocated to different sectors of the aggregate economy as the result of the movement to a stationary population can be rather directly stated. The advent of the stationary age distribution means that there will be relatively more of the aged residing in the population than under a regime of positive population growth. To the extent that private pensions are funded on a pay-as-you-go basis, the onset of zero growth will bring a transfer of current resources from holders of equity capital to the holders of pension rights. While these two groups may not be entirely distinct, we might expect that the transfer will be, on balance, from high savers to low savers as in the Social Security case mentioned previously.

For that portion of aggregate pension rights which is actuarily funded, the situation is somewhat different. Take for a moment the extreme case in which zero population growth, zero economic growth, and a fixed distribution of income all obtain; then, given the definitions that follow,

c(a) = average contribution per capita at age a (a = 20, 64)
B(t) = total benefits in time t
C(t) = total contributions in time t
N(a) = number of individuals aged a

total contributions to the funded pension system in time t will be

$$C(t) = \int_{20}^{64} c(a) \cdot e^{r(64-a)} \cdot N(a)$$

where r is the (fixed) rate of return on pension fund assets, and, as long as the rate of return is greater than zero in a stationary economy, annual benefit payments will exceed annual pension contributions. Thus, in the stationary state, net saving from the funded pension system will be negative. Of course, if the mere existence of the pension system induces additional saving as Cagan and Katona have suggested, the net contribution of the pension system may remain positive.

Economic growth could, if it were rapid enough, result in annual pension contributions which are larger than benefits paid, if the rate of return on capital were independent of the rate of growth of the economy.

On balance, zero population growth will probably lead to a reduction in aggregate saving. To the extent that aggregate saving is too high given the capacity of the economy to maintain full employment, this event might be welcomed; however, if the decline in savings impedes the economy's growth potential, the relative burden on the working population will be higher and the tendencies toward inflation reinforced. In any case, pension saving constitutes over 40 percent of aggregate personal saving and any change in the former will have important consequences for the latter.

SUMMARY AND SOME SUGGESTIONS

The arrival of a stationary population in the United States will be accompanied by a marked increase in the median age of the population and in the ratio of retired to economically active inhabitants. In addition, the growth of aggregate demand for goods and services which is promoted by an increasing population will cease. This chapter has been concerned with the impact that these demographic developments will have on the old age retirement system directly and on the aggregate economy as it is affected by this system.

Given that the Social Security system is funded on a pay-as-you-go basis, the primary impact of zero population growth will be to increase the relative transfer of current goods and services from the working age population to the aged population. We suspect that the net impact of this transfer will be to reduce the relative level of personal saving vis à vis consumption. Ceteris paribus, this implies (1) a decline in the economic growth potential of the economy, and (2) an increase in the rate of growth of the economy needed to maintain the older population without increasing the real burden on the working population. If the history of benefit growth under OASDHI is any indication, real benefits to the aged will increase and so will the real burden on the working population.

Furthermore, the Social Security system may potentially play a significant role in determining the supply of labor in the stationary population economy. As economic growth proceeds in the absence of population growth, potential labor market shortages might develop which would be exacerbated by OASDHI-caused changes in the average retirement age. Either a change in the minimum age at which full benefits can be received or a relaxation in current early retirement privileges might intensify the inflationary pressures deriving from tight labor markets in which excessive market power exists on both the supply and demand sides.

Given the small quantity of information available it would appear that the net addition to aggregate savings generated by pension funds would also be rather reduced on the advent of the stationary state. To the extent that the net addition to saving produced by pension saving in a growing population is inimical to the maintenance of full employment, the arrival of zero population growth will be beneficial. However, aggregate saving might well be too low to maintain the growth in real income which would be desirable in a no-growth population. In that case the role of the government in insuring growth and full employment would have to expand--indeed, an interesting question for future research might be to explore the impact of zero population growth on the necessary magnitude of government intervention in the economy to maintain specified levels of employment and economic growth.

My analysis has been hampered by the lack of information regarding the many ways that population variables affect the macroeconomy. The stagnationist controversies of the 1930s and 1940s as well as the current increase in interest regarding the macroeconomic implications of zero population growth (e.g., Heiser 1973; Leibenstein 1973; Denton and Spencer 1973) suggest that

the time is appropriate for a more systematic inquiry into the
macroeconomic implications of demographic change.

If so, I wish to argue that a line of attack quite distinct
from either short-run neo-Keynesian analyses or long-run neoclassical growth models is essential. The short-run econometric models are inappropriate because the time frame of aggregate demographic changes is considerably longer and the
sorts of questions to be asked are different. Much of what is
assumed to be "structure" in a short-run macro model is in fact
variable in the longer-run economic-demographic context. Likewise, the impact of demographic change on the economic system
is likely to be so pervasive that the highly aggregated neoclassical models are likely to obscure many interrelationships
of interest. Moreover, population is likely to have a strong
impact both on aggregate prices and on the level of unemployment and government intervention in the economy. These are
Keynesian questions placed in a longer-run context and the ac-
quisition of satisfactory answers to them will depend on the
development, testing and simulation of a new class of macroeconomic models which exhibit the long-range framework of the neoclassical approach and the attention to the financial system,
prices, unemployment, and government activity characteristic of
today's neo-Keynesian policy models.

REFERENCES

Aaron, Henry (1966) "The Social Insurance Paradox." *Canadian Journal of Economics* 32:371-74.

Ando, Albert and Modigliani, Franco (1963) "The 'Life Cycle' Hypothesis of Saving: Aggregate Implications and Tests." *American Economic Review* 53:55-84.

Apilado, Vincent (1972) "Pension Funds, Personal Savings and Economic Growth." *Journal of Risk and Insurance* 39:397-404.

Blackburn, John (1967) "The Macroeconomics of Pension Funds," in U.S. Congress, *Old Age Income Assurance*, Part 5.

Board of Governors, Federal Reserve System (1972) *Federal Reserve Bulletin* 58 (June).

Brittain, John (1971) "The Incidence of the Social Security Payroll Tax." *American Economic Review* 61:110-125.

Brown, James Douglas (1972) *An American Philosophy of Social Security: Evolution and Issues*. Princeton, N.J.: Princeton University Press.

Cagan, Phillip (1965) *The Effect of Pension Plans on Aggregate Saving*. New York: National Bureau of Economic Research.

Campbell, C. D. (1969) "Social Insurance in the United States: A Program in Search of an Explanation." *Journal of Law and Economics* 12:249-66.

Denton, Frank and Spencer, Byron (1973) "A Simulation Analysis of the Effects of Population Change on a Neoclassical Economy." *Journal of Political Economy* 81:356-75.

Feldstein, Martin (1972) "The Incidence of the Social Security Payroll Tax: Comment." *American Economic Review* 62:735-38.

Hansen, Alvin H. (1939) "Economic Progress and Declining Population Growth." *American Economic Review* 29:1-15.

Heiser, R. (1973) "The Economic Consequences of Zero Population Growth." *Economic Record* 49:241-62.

Katona, George (1965) *Private Pensions and Individual Saving*. Monograph 40. Ann Arbor, Mich.: Survey Research Center, Institute for Social Research, University of Michigan.

Keynes, John Maynard (1937) "Some Economic Consequences of a Declining Population." *Eugenics Review* 29:13-17.

Leibenstein, Harvey (1973) "The Impact of Population Growth on the American Economy," in Morss and Reed, *Economic Aspects of Population Growth*.

Morss, Elliott R. and Reed, Ritchie H., eds. (1972) *Economic Aspects of Population Change*, Commission on Population Growth and the American Future Research Reports, vol. 2. Washington: U.S. Government Printing Office.

Murray, Roger F. (1968) *Economic Aspects of Pensions: A Summary Report*. New York: National Bureau of Economic Research.

Pechman, Joseph; Aaron, Henry; and Taussig, Michael (1967) "The Objectives of Social Security," in U.S. Congress, *Old Age Income Assurance*, Part 3.

Phelps, Edmund S. (1973) "Some Macroeconomics of Population Levelling," in Morss and Read, *Economic Aspects of Population Change*.

Rejda, George E. (1971) "Social Security and the Paradox of the Welfare State." *Journal of Risk and Insurance* 37:17-39.

_____ and Shepler, Richard J. (1973) "The Impact of Zero Population Growth on the OASDHI Program." *Journal of Risk and Insurance* 40:313-25.

Schoeplein, Robert N. (L970) "The Effect of Pension Plans on Other Retirement Saving." *Journal of Finance* 25:633-37.

Spengler, Joseph J. (1972) "Prospective Population Changes and Price Level Tendencies." *Southern Economic Journal* 38:459-67.

Taylor, Lester D. (1971) "Saving Out of Different Types of Income." *Brookings Papers on Economic Activity*, no. 2:383-415.

U.S. Bureau of the Census (1972) *Current Population Reports: Illustrative Population Projections for the United States: The Demographic Effects of Alternate Paths to Zero Growth*. Ser. P-25, no. 480. Washington: U.S. Government Printing Office.

_____ (1973) *Statistical Abstract of the United States: 1973*. 9th ed. Washington: U.S. Government Printing Office.

U.S. Congress. Joint Economic Committee (1967) *Old Age Income Assurance*. 90th Congress, 1st Session. Washington: U.S. Government Printing Office.

7

Governmental Policy Concerning Population Growth and Distribution in the Piedmont Dispersed City

CHARLES R. HAYES and D. GORDON BENNETT

Dispersed city is a useful phrase to identify the concept of functionally interdependent cities, located in close proximity, but physically separated by nonurban land. Such a city consists of several discrete urban nodes but functions as a single urban entity. That is, dispersed city residents live in one urban node, shop in another, work in a third, seek professional services in yet another and so on. The dispersed city concept is well established in the literature and dispersed cities have been tentatively identified in Ontario, Texas, and Japan as well as in North Carolina.

The nodal interaction, typical of dispersed cities, is generated by actual or perceived internodal specialization. The dispersed city resident perceives one node as the retail mecca, another as the restaurant capital, a third as the employment center, yet another as the medical center, and so on. Obviously, communication is the crux of the matter, if a dispersed city is to function.

A dispersed city is different morphologically from a single-centered city, yet interaction is just as necessary to the polynucleated urban unit as it is to the mononucleated urban unit. That is, people, goods, and information must flow between the several nodes of a dispersed city just as they must between the major and the minor nodes of a single-centered city. Complete communication linkages, however, are more difficult to achieve in a dispersed city because of the greater distances, the nonurban spaces, and the greater number of subnodes involved. (Each node of a dispersed city is a miniature model of a single-centered city and contains a downtown, shopping centers, industrial districts, and so on). There is no identified dispersed city that has solved the transportation problem efficiently. All identified dispersed cities of the world rely heavily on streets, roads, and rubber-tired vehicles for movement.

There have been several suggestions for alleviation of the dispersed city transportation problem: high-speed rail rapid transit along existing thoroughfare medial strips, exclusive bus routes, exclusive bicycle routes, heliports, and other possibilities. None of the suggestions have been completely feasible for one reason or another and few have actually been tried in any dispersed city. The dispersed cities of the world, however, do have one significant plus factor in common. None of them have yet reached a population of much over one million people. Transportational friction is already severe and constantly worsening in the world's dispersed cities, but it is not yet to the point of panic. The alternative to complete an efficient nodal connectivity is population control. The time at which this will become necessary is, however, debatable.

The subject of this chapter, The North Carolina Piedmont Dispersed City (PDC), consists of the major urban nodes of Winston-Salem, Greensboro, High Point, Burlington, Asheboro, and Lexington contained within Forsyth, Guilford, Alamance, Randolph, and Davidson counties (see figure 7.1). We will describe population numbers, growth, and distribution for the Piedmont Dispersed City in general terms and analyze the population planning efforts of the two local organizations that have become publicly involved in considering the population problems of the area. The two protagonists of the case are the Piedmont Triad Council of Governments (COG) and the Greensboro Chamber of Commerce. Although several social scientists, including the authors, have published papers dealing with area problems, recommendations contained in the papers can be rather neatly dichotomized into "population control" vs. "growth is inevitable." COG and the Chamber are the public advocates of these two opposed points of view.

1940-70 GROWTH

Since 1940, the population of the PDC has increased by more than 337,000, or about 77 percent. During the three decades, the growth rates have fluctuated similar to national trends. The 1940s and 1950s had the highest rates, with the 1960s rate dropping to only 62 percent of that of the peak decade of the 1950s.

Not only did the growth rate decline from the 1950s to the 1960s, but the numerical increase was about 40,000 less. Lower birth rates and a lesser net in-migration were the major demographic factors causing this change. Natural increase accounted for about 80 percent of the gain during the last decade.

Figure 7.1. Piedmont Dispersed City

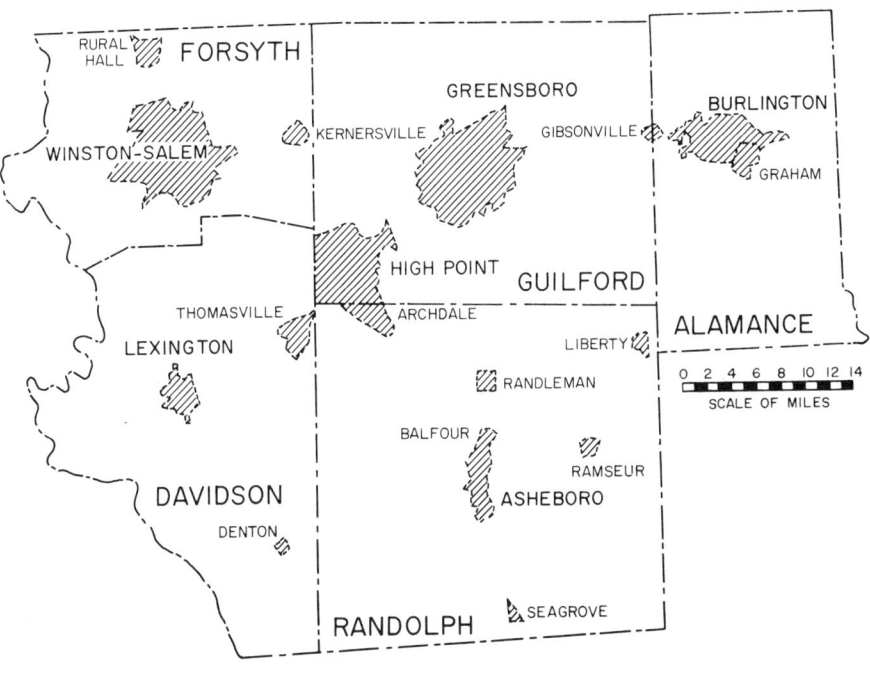

Nevertheless, the PDC did grow more rapidly than 84 of North Carolina's 100 counties (outside the area), the state as a whole, and the nation during the 1960s. However, it increased more slowly than did five of the state's six Standard Metropolitan Statistical Areas (SMSA) outside this area. Relatively slow metropolitan growth in North Carolina is thus already found in the PDC.

Trends in growth rates for the five counties in the PDC have not been parallel with one another. Among these counties, Guilford, the most populous, has ranked second (1940s and 1950s) and third (1960s) in rate of increase, while Forsyth, the second largest has oscillated between next to slowest (1940s and 1960s) and fastest (1950s). During the last three decades, Guilford, Forsyth, and Davidson have followed national trends, with fluctuating rates of growth. Alamance has had declining rates for the three decades, while Randolph has experienced increasing rates.

In the 1960s, the three less populous counties grew by between 10,688 and 14,861, while Forsyth added 26,683 and Guilford, 43,125. Since 1940, Guilford County has had the greatest numerical (134,729) and proportional (89 percent) gains in the PDC. No county in this area has had less than two-thirds increase, however.

As the PDC and its counties have added more people, the densities of the respective units have also become greater. Varying rates of growth have affected the relative densities of the counties. Forsyth, which had a 1940 density 26 percent greater than Guilford, had only a 13 percent higher figure by 1970. Although the three less populous counties have grown considerably since 1950, none of their 1970 densities is more than that of the 1940 figures for either Forsyth or Guilford.

The patterns of population growth within the PDC and its five counties are better indicators of change than total number or density figures. During the last three decades, the urban proportion of the population has risen. An alteration of the definition showed the urban proportion for 1950 to be nearly four percentage points higher than the old definition. Using only the old definition, the PDC had no relative increase in urban people during the 1940s. Only Alamance had a rise in the proportion of urban persons. The percentage of the PDC population living in the six largest towns remained at 48 percent during this time.

The decade of the 1950s was the period of peak growth, as well as the decade of major urban expansion for the PDC. Nearly three-fourths of the PDC increase occurred in the six main cities of the area. Whereas their proportion of the total had not changed during the 1940s, it rose by more than five percentage points to 53 percent during the 1950s. Moreover, the urban share of the population increased from 56 percent (new definition) in 1950 to 62 percent in 1960. A significant amount of annexation accounted for part of this gain, however. Only Davidson County did not follow this pattern; nevertheless, its urban population did grow by 27 percent.

Population growth in the 1960s was smaller and slower than in the previous decade for the PDC and for all six cities and every county, except Randolph. The urban population grew only slightly faster than the rural, so that the urban proportion increased by only 0.1 percentage point. The six largest cities actually grew more slowly than the PDC as a whole, and therefore, accounted for a slightly smaller proportion of the people in 1970 than in 1960. Thus, whereas the numbers of persons in the six largest cities, especially Greensboro and Winston-Salem, and in other urban centers have been rising during the last decade, increases in similar amounts have been occurring in the rural areas surrounding them. In other words, a filling-in of the open spaces between and around urban areas proceeded to a greater extent during the sixties than in the fifties.

1970 POPULATION

In 1970, the population of the PDC was nearly three-quarters of a million. The PDC was the most populous metropolitan area between Washington, D.C., and Atlanta, Georgia, and west to the Ohio-Mississippi Rivers. The density of the PDC is approximately the same as its overlapping SMSA and the SMSAs of Raleigh and Durham, North Carolina; Birmingham, Alabama; and Knoxville, Tennessee, but only 77 percent as dense as the Charlotte, North Carolina, SMSA.

The PDC is 62 percent urban with 53 percent of the people living in the six largest cities. Only one county in the area, Guilford, has a higher proportion of urban people than the nation as a whole, and only two others, Forsyth and Alamance are more urban than the state (45 percent).

The population of the individual counties ranges from over 76,000 in Randolph to nearly 289,000 in Guilford. At present, rather low densities prevail between most of the six major cities, with moderate densities found only between Greensboro and High Point.

1970-2000 PROJECTIONS

The North Carolina Department of Water and Air Resources (DWAR) (based on state projections by the U.S. Office of Business Economics and Economic Research Service [OBERS]), the North Carolina Office of State Planning (OSP), and the Piedmont Triad Council of Governments have developed 1890 population projections for the PDC counties. The DWAR and COG projections are also for the year 2000. The OSP county projections for 1980 are the lowest except for Randolph County. The COG projections for 2000 are usually considerably lower than the DWAR ones. However, the OBERS projections--on which DWAR's are based--and the OSP projections are being revised, most probably downward. Projections now available are given in table 7.1.

The OSP estimates that each county and the PDC will grow slower during the 1970s than the 1960s. However, Guilford and Randolph will have larger numerical gains than in the previous decade, while Davidson, Forsyth, and Alamance will add fewer people than before. The PDC as a whole will have a somewhat smaller numerical growth than in the sixties.

Table 7.1. Population Changes and Projections--North Carolina Piedmont Dispersed City Counties, 1960-2000

County	1960	1970	1960-1970 No.	%	1980	1970-1980 No.	%	2000	1970-2000 No.	%
Alamance	85,674	96,362	10,688	12.5						
DWAR*					108,000	11,638	12.1	136,000	39,638	41.1
OSP**					104,799	8,437	8.8	N.A.	N.A.	N.A.
COG***					110,500	14,138	14.7	127,480	31,118	32.3
Davidson	79,493	95,627	16,134	20.3						
DWAR					115,000	19,373	20.3	161,000	65,373	68.4
OSP					110,674	15,047	15.7	N.A.	N.A.	N.A.
COG					114,290	18,663	19.5	133,380	37,753	39.5
Forsyth	189,428	216,111	26,683	14.1						
DWAR					250,000	33,889	15.7	332,000	115,889	53.6
OSP					235,949	19,838	9.2	N.A.	N.A.	N.A.
COG					248,560	32,449	15.0	319,390	103,279	47.8
Guilford	246,520	288,645	42,125	17.1						
DWAR					340,700	52,055	18.0	475,700	187,055	64.8
OSP					329,988	41,343	14.3	N.A.	N.A.	N.A.
COG					330,240	41,595	14.4	434,490	145,845	50.5
Randolph	61,497	76,358	14,861	24.2						
DWAR					95,000	18,542	24.4	130,000	53,642	70.3
OSP					91,851	15,493	20.3	N.A.	N.A.	N.A.
COG					87,380	11,022	14.4	105,130	28,772	37.7
Piedmont Dispersed City	662,612	773,103	110,491	16.7						
DWAR					908,000	134,897	17.4	1,234,700	461,597	59.7
OSP					873,261	100,158	13.0	N.A.	N.A.	N.A.
COG					890,970	117,867	15.2	1,119,870	346,767	44.9

*DWAR--North Carolina Department of Water and Air Resources, based on U.S. Office of Business and Economics and Economic Research Service (OBERS), 1974.
**OSP --North Carolina Office of State Planning, June 1973.
***COG --Piedmont Triad Council of Governments, January 1975.

The DWAR, on the other hand, projects that during the seventies each county and the PDC will grow approximately as fast, or faster, than during the 1960s; and each will have a greater numerical increase. The gain for the PDC would be 24,400 more than in the last decade.

The COG estimates that Alamance and Forsyth will grow slightly faster in the seventies than in the sixties, but Davidson, Guilford, and Randolph will grow slower. However, the COG projections do show greater numerical gains for all counties, except Randolph, and the PDC during the seventies.

According to the DWAR, from 1980 to 2000, the average annual rates of growth for all counties, except Randolph, and the PDC are expected to be somewhat greater than during the previous two decades. According to the DWAR projections, the PDC will grow by nearly 462,000, or 60 percent, between 1970 and 2000, reaching more than 1.2 million by the end of the century. The density will have increased about 430 persons per square mile, or 22 percent greater than the 1970 density of the Charlotte SMSA.

Rates of growth for the five counties are estimated by DWAR to vary from 41 percent in Alamance County to 70 percent in Randolph. Projected populations for 2000 range from 130,000 to 136,000 and 161,000 for Randolph, Alamance, and Davidson Counties to 332,000 in Forsyth, and 475,000 in Guilford. Randolph would continue to have a fairly low density (162), while Davidson and Alamance would have moderate densities (295 and 313, respectively), and Forsyth and Guilford would have higher densities (783 and 731, in that order).

The COG projections for the year 2000 show much less growth for each of the counties and the PDC, with a total population of slightly over 1.1 million by that date--an increase of nearly 347,000 or almost 45 percent.

Obviously, whichever projections most closely represent the future, the outlook is for over a million persons in the PDC before the year 2000.

Projections for the six major cities of the PDC are not available at the present time. However, LBC & W Associates, together with the Piedmont Triad Council of Governments Staff, have formulated a regional development plan for the year 2000 for an area which includes the PDC. The six cities and other towns are expected to grow both numerically and spatially.

THE COG POSITION

The Piedmont Triad Council of Governments was formed in 1969 to coordinate local planning efforts. COG depends on local acceptance for enforcement of recommendations but retains a professional staff and employs consultants so recommendations for area development are available.

The COG stand on population growth for the five-county area is rather clear cut. COG plans for a constantly declining population growth rate with a goal of equilibrium at 1.1 million persons by the year 2000. COG's position is that a population of this size will not overload facilities as they are improved, in a realistic fashion, over the next three decades. COG points out that present water sources are already adequate for the projected population for the year 2000. COG is currently studying sewer and solid waste management and is confident that these systems will be ready for use as they are needed. The transportation plan is rather vague, but suggests interstate standards for present highways linking the major nodes of the urban system, supplemented by a segment of a state (Charlotte-to-Raleigh) rail rapid transit line along the existing rail right-of-way. The rapid transit system would link Lexington, High Point, Greensboro, and Burlington along the main line, with a spur from Greensboro to Winstom-Salem. The plan suggests improvement of existing airports and additional "strategically located" general aviation airports near any city of 10,000 people. Heliports and intracity buses would round out the transportation system.

The Piedmont Triad Council of Governments proposes to control the population growth of the five county area by controlling industrial in-migration. COG points out that the geographic literature is rich in papers linking population growth to industrial growth in the southern Piedmont. Specific controls for industrial in-migration have not been formulated, but they might be a combination of restrictive zoning, restricted utility services, stiff pollution control regulations for new industry, and tax policy. The Council of Governments sees no real problem in restricting industrial in-migration, if the support of the people and the support of the governmental units of the region can be obtained.

The Council believes that control of population distribution is even more important than control of growth and numbers. COG suggests that the multinodal character of the area be retained. COG argues that Greensboro and Winston-Salem should not be permitted to grow beyond a certain population level, perhaps 250,000; that Burlington, High Point, and Asheboro should be held to smaller populations, perhaps 100,000; and that Lexington and existing smaller cities should contain even fewer people, perhaps only

50,000 each. Population overflow will be diverted to planned "new towns" located within easy auto commuting distances from Greensboro, Winston-Salem, and High Point and to existing smaller cities and towns within the region. In addition, large green belt management areas between urban nodes will preclude obliteration of the physically discrete character of the urban centers. COG believes that urban size, density, and form can be controlled through area-wide zoning, through city boundary control, and through the controlled distribution of utilities and city services.

Planned management green belts present a more difficult problem, according to COG. Some of this land can be purchased and converted to public parks. The bulk of the land, however, must be kept "open" by other means. Area-wide zoning, utility extension policy, tax credits for open land, and the purchase of easements are the methods suggested by COG for retaining green belts.

THE CHAMBER POSITION

The Greensboro Chamber of Commerce, though organized and financed in the typical chamber fashion, is a cut above the usual organization devoted to the needs of local businessmen. The Greensboro Chamber maintains an active urban research division that has produced several very sophisticated publications concerning local and area-wide urban problems. As is the case with COG, both staff and consultants have contributed to the chamber efforts. The Greensboro Chamber of Commerce, then, perceives Greensboro as a unit in a larger city system and is concerned with area-wide urban problems as well as with local urban problems.

The Greensboro Chamber has no objection to the concept of population growth control but it objects to the suggested COG methodology for that growth control. The COG plan to limit population growth by restricting industrial in-migration is anathema to the Chamber. The Chamber points out that only about 20,000 people were added to the urban complex during the past decade by in-migration, while almost 90,000 people were added through an excess of births over deaths. The Chamber believes that to limit jobs through the control of industrial in-migration would force the out-migration of the working age natives, in the Chamber's words: "the contributors--the cream of the crop." The Chamber is adamantly opposed to any policy that might encourage this possibility.

The Chamber claims it does not promote growth, but believes growth is preferable to any suggested alternative, thus inevitable. The Chamber suggests that a 19 percent average population growth rate per decade is reasonable and realistic. At this rate the Piedmont urban complex would reach the 1.1 million mark by 1990 and would total 1.35 million inhabitants by the year 2000. The Chamber agrees with COG that planning, including transportation planning, for 1.1 million people for the five-county area poses no great problem and suggests that a population of this size can be accommodated by 1990. The Chamber position concerning population growth beyond the 1.1 million mark to the year 2000 and beyond is that, by that time, technological breakthroughs will be available to resolve problems that would seem to defy solution today. Who can say, according to the Chamber, what technology for water distribution, sanitation, pollution control, and transportation will be available by 1990? At any rate, the Chamber feels 1990 is soon enough to apply population control should the need arise by then.

The Greensboro Chamber of Commerce agrees with the COG that population distribution is more important than numbers. The Chamber believes, however, that migration will, inevitably, be into the three largest cities: Greensboro, Winston-Salem, and High Point. The Chamber considers this desirable because the proper infrastructure for accommodating large populations is already available in these cities and can readily be expanded to meet future needs and to control distribution within these urban units. The Chamber believes that the physically discrete nature of the urban units of the urban complex can be maintained by developing new towns and by limiting the population of the existing smaller cities and towns in the area. Growth and distribution control is, according to the Chamber, proper for the smaller urban units because the infrastructure is not available in small cities and cannot conceivably be developed in time to control sprawl. The impression would seem to be that the Chamber considers sprawl inevitable, perhaps even desirable, for the larger urban units, but undesirable for the smaller cities and towns of the area.

The Chamber would be delighted with a ring of planned management green belts but considers the concept a "pipe dream" beyond the small amount of land actually purchased. The Chamber points out that zoning has consistently failed in the courts if there is a higher and better use for a large block of land (if it is not spot zoning). The Chamber has considered the possibility of offering tax credits to farmers in the intercity spaces, who do not convert land to urban uses, and pronounces the plan "doomed to failure" According to the Chamber each farmer would accept the credits until offered a high price to convert the land to urban uses. The Chamber predicts that the farmer would then sell the land to the highest bidder. The Chamber has considered the possibility of purchasing 99-year "easements" that require individual farmers to retain land in rural uses, and also pronounces that plan "doomed to failure." According to the Chamber, a farmer in an urbanizing county would be a "fool" to accept a small annual easement payment with potential riches "around the corner." Large payments are not economically feasible and the Chamber does not consider the area farmers fools. The Chamber believes that utility extension policy does not control development, it only controls the direction or location of development. This, too, according to the Chamber, will fail as a method to preserve intercity green belts.

CONCLUSIONS

The two opposed points of view with regard to population planning, as expressed by the Piedmont Triad Council of Governments and the Greensboro Chamber of Commerce probably represent a dichotomy between the administrative bureaucracy and the typical resident of the area. This statement cannot be quantified but interviews with mayors, councilmen, and area planners indicate a positive attitude toward continued population growth for the urban area as symbolized by the Chamber position. On the other hand, residents of the area indicate, by their answers to a multitude of questions, that they favor the COG position. This can be summarized by the factual statement that most residents of the area like living in a "dispersed city," they like it because of its dispersed-city character and they want to keep it that way. COG might promote the "population control" concept with more success if the message could be delivered to the people instead of to the bureaucracy.

8

Population--Energy Requirements, Environmental Effects

CHARLES M. WEISS

THE DILEMMA

Today we are confronted with a dilemma whose magnitude we are just beginning to appreciate and whose final solution will probably not be some major economic maneuver or ecological adjustment but rather a series of small stepwise and incremental changes resulting from sequences of feedback and response. The dilemma is whether population increase can be brought under reasonable control, to hold at some steady state, or whether the energy requirements generated by the increased population as well as the increased per capita demand will impose an excessive burden on the environment. These elements--population, energy, and environment--may be thought of as three sides of a triangle, the dimension of each side still to be determined. The controlling variable in the triangle is not only the size of the population but the consumptive demand of that population. In turn the population and its total energy requirement produce environmental effects. These include not only the waste products of energy production but the irreversible consumption of natural resources.

This dilemma has been examined in numerous conferences which have attempted to establish the guidelines for future generations. However, in spite of our contemporary environmental awareness, we are still confronted with the basic problem. An attempt to assess this problem was highlighted at the 138th American Academy for the Advancement of Science Meeting in Philadelphia, December 1971, where several discussion groups concerned with the future agreed that social and economic institutions as we know them today will have to change to accommodate new economic demands that flow from the energy requirements of a swollen population (C&EN 1972). Added to this is the more recent vision of catastrophe by the Club of Rome warning that certain resources required to sustain our economic growth have physical limits and once used are gone forever (Meadows et al. 1972). But even since the earliest pronouncements by Malthus on limits of society and the computations by Brown (1956) on resources, we are becoming increasingly aware of the dilemma of the triangle, population, energy, environment and the need for an acceptable solution.

ECONOMIC DEVELOPMENT AND ENVIRONMENTAL EFFECTS

The economic model that emphasizes industrialization as the effective force for reducing poverty is probably the most likely mechanism for generating the wealth and resources required to bring environmental effects under control. If we are forced to accept a steady state, a homeostatic system, certain societies will be required to march in place regardless of their state of economic development or level of affluence. It is noteworthy that at the June 1972 Stockholm Conference on the Human Environment, 26 principles were developed and adopted in a worldwide effort at discussion of the problems of economic development and environmental effects (Reuters 1972). These statements are important but they also contain serious contradictions. In attempting to seek a better human environment the conferees tended to ignore the principles by which energy is generated, resources are used, and populations sustained.

The 26 environmental principles of the Stockholm Conference appear in Appendix A to this chapter. The first five principles concern themselves with protection of the environment for future generations, protecting the capacity to produce renewable resources and to prevent the exhaustion of nonrenewable resources. It is stressed that pollution shall be restricted, particularly that of the seas, as well as control of toxic substances and the release of heat so that they do not produce serious or irreversible damage to the ecosystem. However, by the time the drafters of these principles reached number eight, economic and social developments are noted as continuing to be essential to insure a favorable living and working environment for man and for creating the conditions necessary for the improvement of the quality of life. The problems of underdevelopment were noted in principle nine, specifically the questions of the developing countries, the manner in which they would develop their primary commodities and raw materials, essential not only for environmental management, but for the economic factors that are required to insure their growth and well-being. Principle 11 notes that

environmental policies should enhance and not adversely affect
present or future development potential of developing countries;
nor should they hamper the attainment of better living conditions for all (emphasis added). Also appropriate steps should
be taken by states and international organizations to reach an
agreement on meeting possible national and international economic consequences resulting from application of environmental
measures.

The effort at Stockholm was a start even though the questions
of economic development, population growth, and environmental
effects would appear to be on a collision course in terms of
ultimate goals. Another scenario for the future, as reported
by Hazel Henderson (1972), Director of the Council on Economic
Priorities, noted that there may be no realistic hope that presently underdeveloped countries will ever reach the standards of
living the others enjoy as a result of industrialization. In
turn industrialization may be a more fundamentally disturbing
force in world ecology than population, and the highly industrialized societies may be nonsustainable and self-extinguishing.

ENERGY REQUIREMENTS

If the goal of a national economic model is attainment of better
living conditions for all, our contemporary procedures for this
goal call for a substantial energy component. Gerald C. Gambs
indicated the interrelationship of population, energy, environment, and economics in his letter to *The New York Times* 15 October 1971. This letter (Appendix B) serves to illustrate the
relationship between GNP and the energy requirements to support
the GNP in the United States today. As this chapter was being
prepared, the forecasts of the GNP for 1972 and 1973 were published in *The New York Times* (Silk 1972). As of that date the
estimate for 1972 was $1,150 billion and predictions for 1973
ranged from $1,248 to $1,268 billion.

A recent analysis of the energy demand of the United States was
prepared for the Environmental Impact Statement of the proposed
Trans-Alaskan pipeline (SITF 1972). The authors recognized the
relationship between energy demand and the GNP which in turn
was stated as being closely correlated with both population and
per capita income. It followed that the increasing use of energy was noted as correlated with increasing affluence and rising
material standard of living. Their summary of population growth
and energy demands is contained in table 8.1. They recognized
the outlandish per capita consumption increment because the economic cost of energy has not taken into account environmental
cost, resources have been ample, and growth and energy demand

has been little constrained by economic considerations.

Table 8.1. Population Growth and Energy Demands, 1970-2000

Year	Population (millions)		Selected estimates of total energy consumption (trillion BTUs)		Per capita consumption (million BTUs)
	(a)	(b)			
1970	204	204	68,810	68,810	337
1975	216	214	88,612	88,560	410
1985	240	233	133,396	129,548	556
2000	288	256	191,556	170,240	665

SOURCE: U.S. Bureau of Census, 1970: (a) Series D current base forecast; (b) Series X, replacement fertility and no net immigration.

With the industrialization of the United States and the parallel surge of its population, the U.S. economy has always been fueled by cheap energy. Low cost energy has always been an attraction dangled before the industrial market to come and settle or develop a particular area of the country to make use of whatever local resource might be available. An interesting example is seen in North Carolina where the Duke Power Company through its initial development of the "cheap" hydroelectric power on the Catawba River attracted the cotton mills from New England to the Piedmont of North Carolina.

With the coming of the oil age and the internal combustion engine, a network of pipelines for gas and oil has spread its tentacles over the nation, continuing until today to provide energy at a nominal and in retrospect uneconomic cost. However, the prices of fossil fuels have begun to rise, as noted below, and this is only the beginning (Krieger 1972):

	1967	1972
Oil, per barrel	$3.00	$3.50
Natural gas, per 1,000 cu. ft.	0.15	0.45
Coal, per ton	5.00	7.00

It is without question that the consumptive requirement of even a stationary population establishes the nature of its energy requirement. The current demand for energy as developed by the recent historical study on energy growth by the Stanford Research Institute for the Office of Science and Technology is shown in table 8.2.

Table 8.2. End Uses of Energy in the United States Today

Use	Percentage
Transportation	25
Space heating	18
Process steam	16
Direct heat	11
Electric drive	8
Raw materials	6
Water heating	4
Air conditioning	3
Refrigeration	2
Cooking	1
Other	6

SOURCE: Horst and Herendeen (1972).

With rising cost and unavailability of energy in certain forms, industrial production and consumer consumption patterns could radically change. As energy demands have increased the initial reaction has been to build more generating stations, dig more coal, drill more oil wells, and increase refinery capacity. Suddenly the impact of these activities on the environment in the form of air pollution, waste heat discharges, strip mining, and water pollution--to note a few--has become critical. The initial result in the specific instance has been the demand for limitations on high sulfur, coal, and oil. The quantities of these desirable fuels are limited and not always in the right place from a consumption point of view.

The earlier promise of nuclear energy has been systematically stalled for technical reasons as well as environmental concern, but if the order books are any indication, a significant energy requirement will surely be met by these "clean" power generators. However, even the nuclear plant requires fuel and the estimated recoverable 270,000 tons of uranium ore from U.S. sources place a limit on conventional nuclear energy from light-water reactors for the near term. In the immediate future, the next 10 to 20 years, the domestic energy supply adds to the following: inadequate supplies of oil and gas, coal in the wrong form or prohibited from use, and nuclear energy generators delayed to a point where they won't be ready in time or in sufficient numbers to take up the slack in electric power generation.

All energy demand studies have indicated no imminent decline in requirement for energy. Between 1960 and 1970 increase was on the order of 50 percent. The energy group of the Chase Manhattan Bank in its estimate of energy in the U.S. for 1985 notes that per capita use has doubled in the past 30 years and that it will continue to grow at even a faster rate is clearly indicated. This pessimistic outlook for near-term energy demand is intimately linked with population growth and a rising standard of living. Even at a minimum of growth of 1-1.5 percent per year, the U.S. population will by the year 2000 approach 280 million. Even if no change of per capita consumption were to take place, the population growth itself would expand energy demand. In fact the opposite is indicated--per capita consumption will not hold steady but rather increase. The Census Bureau estimates that one-third of the total population increase between now and 1985 will be in the 25-34 age group. An additional 27 million people will be in their twenties, thirties, and early forties compared to an increase of only 2 million in the number of people between 45 and 64. It is this younger age group, in which marriages, household formations, and births take place, that the need for goods and services requiring energy will expand.

Per capita energy consumption has been noted as correlating closely with standard of living as exemplified by gross national product. If the social goal of a continuing rise in the standard of living for more and more of our citizens is pursued, per capita energy consumption will rise. Improvement of quality of life through environmental control adds additional energy demand per capita. To purify sewage requires energy just as energy is required to purify stack emissions from power generating plants.

The development of new technologies for producing energy as well as new energy sources will inevitably be accelerated to take up the slack as old sources and techniques become obsolete. We will have to develop a new consciousness of energy conservation, to wave a new flag as the environmentalists did in 1968 and 1969. Some of the conservation that would result from a simple awareness of the value and real economic cost of energy is illustrated in the following example. It is estimated that if proper insulation was installed in all houses in the United States, more than 20 billion gallons of oil or more than 1 trillion cubic feet of natural gas could be saved every year. Included in this awareness would be the more efficient use of air conditioning, a reduction in the movement of freight from trucks back to rail, the greater use of intercity passenger traffic from air to rail and bus, and the expanded use by urban commuters of mass transit. Such shifts away from a wasteful use of energy has been estimated as reducing our oil demands by an equivalent 7.3 million barrels per day.

The Southeastern United States has been one of the more rapidly growing areas of the country for the recent decade. With it has been the accelerated use of energy not only to provide for the increase in industrialization but the consumptive uses, particularly air conditioning. The order of magnitude of projected electrical energy requirement is seen in table 8.3.

Table 8.3. Installed Capacity--Megawatts (FPC Estimates) for 17 Southern States

Generator	1970	1980	1990
Fossil steam	115,183	194,204	315,430
Nuclear	700	65,674	193,133
Other	13,956	24,960	34,629
Total	129,839	284,838	543,192

These electrical energy requirements and the lead times required for construction, as well as the state of art of power generation, will require 100 new fossil fuel plants and 96 new nuclear plants for the 17 southern states to meet the projected demand. The location of these plants with reference to their load centers as well as technical requirements for dumping excess heat will impose severe environmental constraints on site selection and the requirements for proper land use.

In the short-term perspective, 25-50 years, the technically affluent societies can probably make the necessary adjustments in energy production technology to meet their demands. Even with stabilization or reduction in per capita demand, the total environmental impact may be severe unless extreme conservatism is established in the use of nonrenewable resources. A current contradiction is the emission control requirements for automobile engines which will increase fuel consumption by 10-15 percent in the 1975 models. The Office of Emergency Preparedness has noted that this increment in fuel consumption could seriously deplete fuel reserves (BW 1972).

In the perspective of a century it is quite clear that the large populations of the "underdeveloped world" will be unable to develop the energy commodity necessary to raise their standards of living. They may now be closer to an equilibrium condition with their environment and in a better condition to survive the energy crisis that industrialized nations will inevitably face.

POSTSCRIPT: THE SITUATION LATE IN 1974

Within one year of writing this chapter the dilemma posed by the energy-environment-population triangle was suddenly brought into sharp focus by the October War of 1973, in the middle East. The subsequent and continuing energy crisis due initially to the oil embargo and then the inflated price on oil, as set by the cartel of the OPEC (Organization of Petroleum Exporting Countries), increased the strain on the triangle. A spreading worldwide famine exacerbated in energy poor countries and thrust into even sharper focus that limits to the dimensions of the triangle had been reached (McElheny 1974). Continued growth of energy or population would lead to environmental costs, a consequence in part of increased energy production, that might prove burdensome for even an affluent society (WSJ Staff Reporter 1974; Schorr 1974; Bird 1974; Singer 1974; Wolozin 1974b).

The cost of developing what had appeared to be promising alternate energy sources is already proving to be uneconomic, even in competition with the inflated price of oil. The alternative, it is argued, has to be conservation (Ford Foundation 1974). This in turn has brought the counter argument that what was being asked.is not conservation but rationing with the consequence of a sharp reduction in living standards (Mobil Oil Corp. 1974). We are rapidly approaching a decision point that has appeared much sooner than expected, forced in part by the unrealistic price of oil as well as the demand that available sources of fossil fuel energy for central power stations be restricted (for example, coal with high sulfur content) or that uneconomic unproven techniques of sulfur removal be forced onto an energy system already becoming cost burdensome to many economic groups for their daily energy requirements.

Still other determinations indicate that the level of per capita energy consumption in the United States, postulated as a direct relationship to the GNP, could be trimmed significantly without major impact on our life style (Mazur and Rosa 1974). Although economic indicators were found to be consistently highly associated with energy consumption, it is suggested that after an initial short-term period of adjustment, linked to highly motivated commitments to conserve energy, the pressure on the energy-environment-population triangle would be substantially relieved.

In advanced technological societies it will also be necessary in the next two to three decades to substantially expand energy and to minimize wasteful uses. This may be accomplished not only by intensive exploration for and development of fossil fuel resources, but also by a shift away from space heating and cooling in buildings using such fuels. A substantial development of solar heating units for home and commercial buildings will provide the principal sources of energy for heating, cooling, and hot water. A major change will be in the increased production of coal primarily for central power station fuel, gasification, and liquid petroleum production. Nuclear power reactors will be providing an increasing proportion of the electrical base load with breeder reactors and finally nuclear fusion becoming technically feasible for commercial use. A movement back to the central city with increased use of mass transit will also bring out a substantial reduction in wasteful uses of fuel for personal transportation (Lee 1974).

Achievement of a state of national energy independence, for essentially all countries, will require not only development of all reasonable sources of energy, concomitant with geographical location and available resources, but the latter will have to be developed at a true economic cost, which will include reasonable environmental controls. The third side of the triangle, the consumers of energy require that not only their numbers be limited but per capita demands become increasingly conservative.

APPENDIX A

from the New York Times, Saturday, June 17, 1972

TEXT OF THE ENVIRONMENTAL PRINCIPLES

STOCKHOLM. *June 16 (Reuters)--Following is the statement of principles from the Declaration on the Human Environment adopted by the United Nations Conference on the Human Environment.*

[1] Man has the fundamental right to freedom, equality and adequate conditions of life, in an environment of a quality which permits a life of dignity and well-being, and bears a solemn responsibility to protect and improve the environment for present and future generations. In this respect, policies promoting or perpetuating apartheid, racial segregation, discrimination, colonial and other forms of oppression and foreign domination stand condemned and must be eliminated.

[2] The natural resources of the earth including the air, water, land, flora and fauna and especially representative samples of natural ecosystems must be safeguarded for the benefit of present and future generations through careful planning or management as appropriate.

[3] The capacity of the earth to produce vital renewable resources must be maintained and wherever practicable restored or improved.

[4] Man has a special responsibility to safeguard and wisely manage the heritage of wildlife and its habitat which are now gravely imperiled by a combination of adverse factors. Nature conservation including wildlife must therefore receive importance in planning for economic developments.

[5] The nonrenewable resources of the earth must be employed in such a way as to guard against the danger of their future exhaustion and to insure that benefits from such employment are shared by all mankind.

[6] The discharge of toxic substances or of other substances and the release of heat, in such quantities of concentrations as to exceed the capacity of the environment to render them harmless, must be halted in order to insure that serious or irreversible damage is not inflicted upon ecosystems. The just struggle of the peoples of all countries against pollution should be supported.

[7] States shall take all possible steps to prevent pollution of the seas by substances that are liable to create hazards to human health, to harm living resources and marine life, to damage amenities or to interfere with other legitimate uses of the sea.

[8] Economic and social development is essential for insuring a favorable living and working environment for man and for creating conditions on earth that are necessary for the improvement of the quality of life.

[9] Environmental deficiencies generated by the conditions of underdevelopment and natural disasters pose grave problems and can be remedied by accelerated development through the transfer of substantial quantities of financial and technological assistance as a supplement to the domestic effort of the developing countries and such timely assistance as may be required.

[10] For the developing countries, stability of prices and adequate earnings for primary commodities and raw material are essential to environment management since economic factors as well as ecological processes must be taken into account.

[11] The environmental policies of all states should enhance and not adversely affect the present or future development potential of developing countries, nor should they hamper the attainment of better living conditions for all, and appropriate steps should be taken by states and international organizations with a view to reaching agreement on meeting the possible national and international economic consequences resulting from the application of environmental measures.

[12] Resources should be made available to preserve and improve the environment, taking into account the circumstances and particular requirements of developing countries and any costs which may emanate from their incorporating environmental safeguards into their development planning and the need for making available to them, upon their request, additional international technical and financial assistance for this purpose.

[13] In order to achieve a more rational management of resources and thus to improve the environment, states should adopt an integrated and coordinated approach to their development planning so as to insure that development is compatible with the need to protect and improve the human environment for the benefit of their population.

[14] Rational planning constitutes an essential tool for reconciling any conflict between the needs of development and the need to protect and improve the environment.

[15] Planning must be applied to human settlements and urbanization with a view to avoiding adverse effects on the environment and obtaining maximum social economic and environmental benefits for all. In this respect projects which are designed for colonialist and racist domination must be abandoned.

[16] Demographic policies, which are without prejudice to basic human rights and which are deemed appropriate by governments concerned, should be applied in those regions where the rate of population growth or excessive population concentrations are likely to have adverse effects in the environment or development, or where low population density may prevent improvement of the human environment and impede development.

[17] Appropriate national institutions must be entrusted with the task of planning, managing or controlling the environmental resources of states with the view to enhancing environmental quality.

[18] Science and technology, as part of their contribution to economic and social development must be applied to the identification, avoidance and control of environmental risks and the solution of environmental problems and for the common good of mankind.

[19] Education in environmental matters, for the younger generation as well as adults, giving due consideration to the underprivileged, is essential in order to broaden the basis for an enlightened opinion and responsible conduct by individuals, enterprises and communities in protecting and improving the environment in its full human dimension. It is also essential that mass media of communications avoid contributing to the deterioration of the environment, but, on the contrary, disseminate information of an educational nature on the need to protect and improve the environment in order to enable man to develop in every respect.

[20] Scientific research and development in the context of environmental problems, both national and multinational, must be promoted in all countries, especially the developing countries. In this connection, the free flow of up-to-date scientific information and experience must be supported and assisted to facilitate the solution of environmental problems: environmental technologies should be made available to developing countries on terms which would encourage their wide dissemination without constituting an economic burden on the developing countries.

[21] States have, in accordance with the Charter of the United Nations and the principles of international law, the sovereign

right to exploit their own resources pursuant to their own environmental policies, and the responsibility to insure that activities within their jurisdiction or control do not cause damage to the environment of other states or of areas beyond the limits of national jurisdiction.

[22] States ahall cooperate to develop further the international law regarding liability and compensation for the victim of pollution and other environmental damage caused by activities within the jurisdiction or control of such states to areas beyond their jurisdiction.

[23] Without prejudice to such general principles as may be agreed upon by the international community, or to the criteria and minimum levels which will have to be determined nationally, it will be essential in all classes to consider the systems of values prevailing in each country, and the extent of the applicability of standards which are valid for the most advanced countries but which may be inappropriate and of unwarranted social cost for the developing countries.

[24] International matters concerning the protection and improvement of the environment should be handled in a cooperative spirit by all countries, big or small, on an equal footing. Cooperation through multilateral or bilateral arrangements or other appropriate means is essential to prevent, eliminate or reduce and effectively control adverse environmental effects resulting from activities conducted in all spheres, in such a way that due account is taken of the sovereignty and interests of all states.

[25] States shall insure that international organizations play a coordinated, efficient and dynamic role for the protection and improvement of the environment.

[26] Man and his environment must be spared the effects of nuclear weapons and all other means of mass destruction. States must strive to reach prompt agreement, in the relevant international organs, on the elimination and complete destruction of such weapons.

APPENDIX B

from The New York Times/October 15, 1971

LIMITS ON THE G.N.P.

To the Editor:

The recent forecast of the 1972 G.N.P. by the National Association of Business Economists sounds like another "Alice in Wonderland" look at the future. I believe that it will be impossible for the G.N.P. to reach $1,143 billion in 1972 ($782 billion in 1958 dollars) for one single reason: There will not be enough energy to allow the U.S. to reach that level by 1972.

Total Energy Consumption--USA, 1966-1972

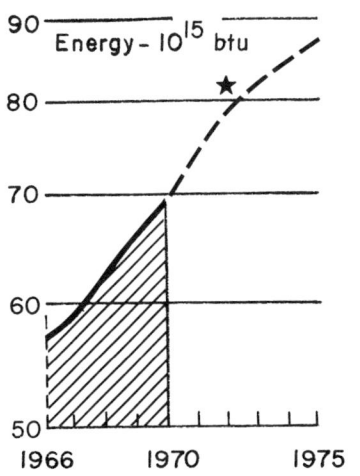

★ Indicated energy requirement if GNP is to reach $1,143 billion in 1972.

— — — Probable maximum energy available and therefore will restrict GNP in 1972 to about $1,100 billion.

The total energy consumption in the U.S.A. in the past five years (1966-70) has been increasing at an average rate of 5.1 per cent per year. If the G.N.P. forecast by the economists for 1972 is to be reached it will require an estimated increase of 11 per cent in energy consumption for that year. My revised estimate shows instead an increase of 6.7 per cent in energy consumption. The ratio of energy to the G.N.P. 1958 dollar, calculated at 86,500 B.T.U.s per (1958) dollar in 1966, will rise to an estimated 105,000 B.T.U.'s per dollar in 1972, when total energy consumption will be an estimated trillion B.T.U.'s.

Because of the current shortage of fossil fuels, coal, oil and gas, and because of the slowdown in the construction and operation of all power plants but particularly nuclear power plants, it is my opinion that it will be impossible for the economy to reach the levels which are being projected for 1972, and the shortage of electric generating capacity and the shortage of fuels will be the restraining and limiting factors. I estimate a G.N.P. of $1,100 billion for 1972 as the maximum based on availability of energy.

Gerald C. Gambs

New York, Oct. 4, 1971

The writer is director of special projects for Ford, Bacon & Davis, Inc.

REFERENCES

Barkley, Paul W. and Seckler, David W. (1972) *Economic Growth and Environmental Decay: The Solution Becomes the Problem.* New York: Harcourt Brace Jovanovich.

Berkowitz, David A. and Squires, Arthur M., eds. (1971) *Power Generation and Environmental Change.* Cambridge, Mass.: MIT Press.

Bezdek, Roger and Hannon, Bruce (1974) "Energy, Manpower and the Highway Trust Fund." *Science* (23 August):669-75.

Bird, David (1974) "Controls on Con Ed, Luce Charges, Pose Question of Sanity." *The New York Times* (23 August):60.

Brown, Harrison (1956) "Technological Denudation," in *Man's Role in Changing the Face of the Earth,* edited by William L. Thomas, Jr. Chicago: University of Chicago Press.

Brown, Theodore L. (1971) *Energy and the Environment.* Columbus, O.: Charles E. Merrill.

BW (1972) "Detroit Locks in on Its Cleanup Methods." *Business Week* (25 November):68-69.

C&EN (1972) "Scientists Plumb the Unknowable Future." *Chemical and Engineering News* (10 January):27-28.

Committee on Power Plant Siting, National Academy of Engineering (1972) *Engineering for Resolution of the Energy-Environment Dilemma.* Washington: National Academy of Engineering.

Energy Policy Project Staff. *A Time to Choose: America's Energy Future.* Energy Policy Project of the Ford Foundation. Lexington, Mass.: Ballinger Books

Ford Foundation Energy Policy Project (1974) *Exploring Energy Choices. A Preliminary Report of the Ford Foundation's Energy Policy Project.* Washington: The Ford Foundation Energy Policy Project.

Garvey, Gerald (1972) *Energy, Ecology, Economy.* New York: Norton.

Hammond, Allen L.; Metz, William D.; and Maugh, Thomas H., II (1973) *Energy and the Future.* Washington: American Association for the Advancement of Science.

Henderson, Hazel (1972) "Economists vs. Ecologists." *The New York Times* (24 October):14

Holmes, Jay, ed. (1973) *Energy, Environment, Productivity. Proceedings of the First Symposium on RANN: Research Applied to National Needs*. Washington: National Science Foundation.

Horst, Eric and Herendeen, Robert (1972) "A Diet Guide for Chronic Energy Conservatives." *Saturday Review* (28 October): 64-66.

Komanoff, Charles; Miller, Holly; and Noyes, Sandy (1972) *The Price of Power, Electric Utilities and the Environment*. New York: The Council on Economic Priorities.

Krieger, James H. (1972) "Energy: The Squeeze Begins." *Chemical and Engineering News* (13 November):20-37.

Lee, James E. (1974) "Longer Range Viewpoints on Energy." *The Futurist* 8:243-44.

Lessing, Lawrence (1972) "The Coming Hydrogen Economy." *Fortune* 86(5):138-46.

Mazur, Alland and Rosa, Eugene (1974) "Energy and Life Style." *Science* (15 November):607-10.

McIlheny, Victor K. (1974) "Rising World Fertilizer Scarcity Threatens Famine for Millions." *The New York Times* (1 September):1.

Meadows, Donella H.; Meadows, Dennis L.; Randers, Jørgen; and Behrens, William W., III (1972) *The Limits to Growth. A Report for the Club of Rome's Project on the Predicament of Mankind*. New York: Universe Books. A Potomac Associates Book.

Mobil Oil Corp. (1974) "A Time to Choose. Energy Growth or Economic Stagnation." *The New York Times* (18 October):41.

Reuters (1972) "Text of Environmental Principles." *The New York Times* (17 June):2.

Schorr, Burt (1974) "EPA Eases Rules for Electric Utilities, But It Says Water Quality Won't Be Hurt." *Wall Street Journal* (26 September):8.

Schurr, Sam H., ed. (1972) *Energy, Economic Growth and the Environment*. Baltimore: Johns Hopkins Press.

Silk, Leonard (1971) "Economic Forecaster on Target." *The New York Times* (15 November):4.

Singer, S. F. (1974) "Emission Standards: Costs and Benefits." *Science* (22 November):689.

SITF *(1972)* "Alternatives to the Proposed Action." *Final Environmental Impact Statement, Proposed Trans-Alaska Pipeline*. Prepared by a Special Interagency Task Force for the Federal Task Force on Alaskan Oil Development. Vol. 5 Washington: The Department of the Interior.

Starr, Chauncey et al. (1971) "Energy and Power." *Scientific American* 225(3):37ff.

U.S. Congress, Joint Committee on Atomic Energy. (1970) *Environmental Effects of Producing Electric Power*. Hearings before the Joint Committee, 91st Cong., 2d sess., 1970, Part 2. 2 vols. Washington: U.S. Government Printing Office.

WSJ Staff Reporter (1974) "Utility Firms Dispute EPA Cost Estimates on Clean Water Plan." *Wall Street Journal* (27 June): 24.

Wolozin, Harold, ed. (1974a) *The Economics of Pollution*. Morristown, N.J.: General Learning Corp.

_____ (1974b) *Energy and the Environment: Selected Readings*. Morristown, N.J.: General Learning Corp.

9

Characteristics and Needs of an Aging Population in a Southern Metropolitan Area

VIRA R. KIVETT

The total population of the United States has tripled its size since 1900 (Williams 1970). During the same 70-year span, the older population increased sevenfold. The population group aged 65 years or more totaled 20 million in 1971, and by the year 2000, it is estimated that it will number approximately 25 million (U.S. Government 1973b).

Achievements in longevity, while desired and welcomed, present somewhat of a crisis to our social structure as it exists today. Efforts are currently being made to restructure national policies in order that society can accommodate the needs of the growing number of older Americans. The second White House Conference on Aging held in December, 1971, pointed out many needs of the older population and made recommendations for meeting them (see U.S. Government 1973a and 1973b). As a result, new national policies toward older people are being formed and action on numerous recommendations from the Conference has occurred. We are entering a period of time when many unmet needs of the older population may be the results of a local government's: (1) lack of knowledge regarding the needs of its older population or available resources to meet these needs; (2) lack of coordination of existing services within the region; or (3) inefficient referral systems.

Certain needs and problems of the aging are national or universal in scope. But, some needs vary according to a number of factors which include regionality, race, or degree of urbanization. As a result, the needs of older people must be investigated and alternative solutions explored according to locale, or otherwise programs born out of new administrative policies will not be wholly effective.

An intensive survey of the characteristics, needs, and sources of assistance of persons aged 65 years or older was conducted in Guilford County, North Carolina during 1970-72.[1] Data from the survey were used in this chapter (Kivett, Bishop, and Watson 1973). The major purposes of this chapter are twofold: (1) to describe selected characteristics and problems of persons 65 years or older who were living in a southern metropolitan area, and (2) to discuss resources for meeting some of the more pressing needs of the older population.

OVERVIEW OF THE STUDY

Population Characteristics

Guilford County, the area selected for the study, is located within the North Carolina Piedmont Triad, an area classified as a Standard Metropolitan Statistical Area (SMSA) by the U.S. Bureau of the Census (1970). The county is second largest of 100 counties in North Carolina and it encompasses two of the state's largest cities, Greensboro, population approximately 144,000, and High Point, population approximately 62,200. The remaining municipalities in the county are Gibsonville, 2,019, and Jamestown, 1,297. Guilford County is one of 11 counties forming the Piedmont Triad Council of Governments, a multiplanning regional structure. Guilford is one of five counties composing the Piedmont Dispersed City (PDC), an urban nodal concept described in this publication by Hayes and Bennett (chap. 7). A dispersed city is made up of several discrete urban nodes (located in close proximity), but the "city" functions as a single entity.

The number of persons 65 or older in Guilford County showed a 48.8 percent increase between 1960 and 1970 (U.S. Bureau of the Census 1970). Persons 65 years or older in 1970 constituted approximately 8 percent of the total county population. The figures projected for the year 2000 show an overall increase of 34.1 percent over the 23,363 older persons living in Guilford County in 1970 (APS 1973).

A breakdown of the projection shows that the degree of increase among older people between the years 1970 and 2000 will vary according to sex and race. Whereas a 26.4 percent increase among the older black population is expected, an increase of 41.1 percent is projected for older whites. Dramatic distinctions in rates of increase are projected for males and females. A 53.5 percent increase among older females is predicted as compared to a 4.2 percent increase in older males (APS 1973). This projection greatly magnifies the known male-female mortality differential in the population.

While the percentage of increase in older people in Guilford County is predicted to decline between 1970 and the year 2000, numerically the number of aging will increase by 118,081 (APS 1973). An accession of 118,081 older individuals is significant when viewed from the standpoint that a majority of persons in age groups of 65 and above are past their peak in earning power, limited in health and strength, and increasingly less able to cope with a rapidly moving world.

Sample

The sample selection for this study was based upon a randomized procedure using clustered census tracts. A compact sampling method was employed within each of the selected sampling units (every eligible household within the selected tract was sampled).

The study was designed to insure the inclusion of as many types of older residents of Guilford County as possible. The sampling rate approximated the proportion of older people in the population and yielded a total of 469 persons 65 years or older. Separate randomized selections were made among rural, urban, and group quartered persons.[2] Surrogate respondents (family member, friend, or nurse) were interviewed in the place of the incapacitated elderly in order to insure their representation in the study.

Ages for the 469 subjects ranged from 65 to 99 with a median age of 72 years. Social position was determined through the use of Hollingshead's two factor index of social position (Hollingshead 1965), the scores of which are based upon educational and occupational backgrounds. The social position of the majority of the sample, 77.7 percent, was characterized by working class backgrounds. Sample proportions approximated those in the population in regard to race and sex (table 9.1).

The overall median educational level of the sample was 7.4 years. This level approximated that previously shown for Piedmont Triad white males and was from one to two years greater than the corresponding figure for black males and females in the population (U.S. Bureau of the Census 1970). The median educational level for white females 65 years or older in the population was higher than the overall median found for this survey sample.

Occupation at age 50 was the point of reference for occupational type. Data showed that approximately 71 percent of the sample fell into the skilled manual, machine operator, farmer, housewife and unskilled occupation categories. Married couples constituted the largest marital status category, 53.2 percent; followed by the widowed, 36.1 percent; and the never married, 7.3 percent. The majority of older people, 63.8 percent, reported themselves as family heads.

Table 9.1. Population Parameters and Sample Characteristics of Persons 65 Years or Older According to Race and Sex

Characteristic	Percentages	
	Population	Sample
Race		
White	80.0	75.0
Black	20.0	25.0
Sex		
Male	37.2	37.7
Female	62.8	62.3

Questionnaire

A questionnaire containing 104 items of information was administered to the subjects by trained interviewers. Included on the questionnaire were items relative to demographic data, housing status and preferences; work status and satisfaction; health status; visiting patterns with children, siblings, and neighbors; income; medical costs; leisure time activities; problems and worries; and life satisfaction. Surrogate respondents answered only factual type questions. Items on the questionnaire reflected the coordinated efforts of a number of agencies in the area who assisted in its planning. Cooperating agencies included the local Health Department, Department of Social Services, Council on Aging, Cooperative Extension Service, and the Social Security Administration.

Statistical Procedures

Procedures affording both descriptive and inferential interpretation were utilized in the study.[3] Data described here used descriptive statistics as well as analysis of variance, regression analysis, and t tests.

General Findings

Housing. Approximately one in every two older adults owned their own home, mortgage free. When respondents were asked if they had ever thought about moving from their present housing arrangement, 83.2 percent said no. About seven in 10 of the respondents reported that they had not moved within the past five years and they were most likely to have lived in the same neighborhood or community for 30 years or more. When confronted with the question dealing with their preference for alternate housing in the event that it became necessary, one in every two older people preferred a one-story apartment rather than a high rise apartment, nursing home, or mobile home. Respondents generally preferred to live apart from, but near, relatives.

Employment. About four in every five of the older people interviewed were fully retired. Retirees had been retired for an average of seven years, and they usually had retired because of poor health (51 percent). Feelings about retirement ranged from liking it very much (41.1 percent) to disliking it very much (31.8 percent). The usual answer given for disliking retirement was the loss of routine working habits.

A small percentage of older adults (7.3 percent) was still employed full time. Part-time work was held by 13.3 percent of the sample who usually reported that they enjoyed their work very much. Older people who were working part-time generally worked because they felt that working was better for them physically and mentally than inactivity in retirement. Only one in four persons who were employed part-time expressed plans to ever fully retire.

Income. The gross annual incomes of older adults ranged from $50 to $65,000, with only eight persons reporting incomes of over $10,000. The mean annual income per older person (exclusive of the eight over $10,000) was $2,307.66. The primary source of income for nine in every 10 persons 65 years or older was Social Security benefits. Savings and investments were income sources for approximately one-half of the respondents. Relatives were seldom sources of regular financial assistance.

Older people, when asked about the adequacy of their income, generally indicated that they had sufficient money if they were careful (43.4 percent). Inadequate incomes were reported by 27.1 percent of older adults who stated that they did not have enough money to meet their needs. Areas in which income was inadequate were: (1) housing, cost and maintenance; (2) clothing; (3) medical care; (4) food; (5) furnishings; (6) transportation; and (7) recreation. Inadequacy of income was more prevalent among the black segment of the population and among persons from a low social position (education and occupation).

Family. The median number of living children per older person interviewed was 2.3. The majority of older parents (70.6 percent) had at least one child living in the same town or county with them. One in every two respondents reported a daily contact with at least one child. Some geographical mobility of children was noted among 44.1 percent of the older parents who said that they had one or more children who lived over 250 miles from Guilford County. There was an equal exchange of visits between parents and children.

Respondents usually reported at least two living brothers or sisters. Half of the sample had at least one sibling who lived in Guilford County. Visits with local brothers and sisters were usually on a weekly or monthly basis and visits were equally exchanged.

General Problems. Respondents were asked, "What do you consider to be your biggest problems or worries?" The major problem of the elderly (63.9 percent) was health. Other problems of important concern to about one in four older people were making ends meet, money in old age, and the world situation. Problems mentioned, but of less magnitude, were suitable housing, keeping a job, and family problems.

A number of areas such as finances, health, and loneliness were listed and older people were asked to indicate the extent to which these areas gave them trouble. The majority of older people indicated that they seldom worried. Transportation was a problem "sometimes" to about one in two older adults. Other areas that were worries "sometimes" to respondents (as indicated by approximately 15 percent) were energy, money, and nerves.

The extent to which older people experienced trouble in areas such as health, housing, transportation, free time, energy, and diet was related to several population characteristics. Residence, sex, race, age, and education were associated with the extent of problems encountered in late life. Fewer problems were reported by older people who were urban rather than rural, male rather than female, and white rather than black. There was more concern with problems when respondents were 80 or more years of age and when persons had received only an elementary school education rather than a high school or college education. Problems in later life were less pronounced among urban white males than among other urban segments, and in the rural areas, white females reported less concern with problems than black females.

Concern with day-to-day problems increased as several factors in the population increased. Concerns increased with poor health, free time, inadequate income, and with feelings of the unimportance of religion.

Health. When asked to rate their own health in terms of good, fair, or poor, older adults were most likely to report "fair" (42 percent). One in every three rated their health as good, and slightly more than one in four reported poor health. Race was associated with the way in which older people rated their health. Blacks rated their health poorer than whites. Poorer health ratings were also found to increase among persons of a low social position.

The majority of the respondents (81.6 percent) reported that they had one or more health problems. Among the bodily ailments reported, arthritis and rheumatism were more frequent than other ailments, and they were reported by about half the sample. Other of the more prominent disabilities were blood pressure irregularities, problems involving the eyes, heart trouble, and nerves.

Most respondents (57.4 percent) reported that they took regular medication for their health problems. A few of the aging (17.7 percent) said that they "just lived with their problems and accepted them." Better than one-half of older Guilfordians (50.8 percent) had visited a doctor during the past year, and the most frequent reason for a medical visit was for a check-up (71.4 percent).

Better than one-half of the respondents (57.2 percent) indicated that their health had caused them to curtail some of their activities during the past year. However, three in every four older persons reported that they were usually mobile to the point of going practically anywhere they wanted to go. Less than four percent of older adults were confined to a chair or a bed most of the time. Hospitalization during the previous year was reported by about one in every five older persons and medican expenses during the 12-month period prior to the study averaged $368.83 per person.[4]

Unhappiness. When older people were asked how much unhappiness they found in life, they most frequently reported "almost none" (60.4 percent). Some unhappiness was reported by 24 percent, followed by 15.7 percent who acknowledged a great deal.

Unhappiness was associated with several population characteristics. Rural older people expressed significantly more unhappiness than urban people, and widows indicated more unhappiness than married people. Persons with limited education (0-2 years) revealed more unhappiness than those with slightly more education (3-5 years or 6-8 years). Unhappiness increased with inadequate income and with the unimportance of religion.

Religion was considered to be the "most important thing" in the lives of more than half the respondents. About one in four older people considered maintaining a spiritual relationship with God to be their most important purpose in life. "Helping others" was the most important purpose for one in three older adults.

Services Needed

Respondents were asked what services should be made available to help with the needs of older people. A service to help with health problems was a prominent need voiced by older Guilfordians (table 9.2). Finances and housing were two other main areas in which the majority of respondents felt services to older persons should be available.

Table 9.2. Services Desired for Older Adults as Reported by Persons 65 Years or Older*

Service	Percent
Health	73.8
Finances	69.5
Housing	65.5
Food	61.6
Help to meet new friends	60.1
Legal assistance	59.7
Employment	58.1
Recreation	57.4
Education	47.1
Family	45.2
Other	5.3

*Multiple responses

A question that dealt with knowledge of available services revealed that the majority of older people in the county were unaware of many existing sources of assistance and information. Familiarity with sources of assistance was less with newer programs such as Meals on Wheels, Home Health Aid Service, Council on Aging, and the Economic Opportunity Program. Services attached to the Social Security Administration (Medicare and Social Security benefits) had been used more frequently than other sources of assistance.

DISCUSSION

Data from a study of 469 people aged 65 years and older who were living in Guilford County, North Carolina, provided valuable insight into important characteristics and needs of an aging metropolitan population. Information from local surveys such as the one reported here can play a valuable role in the comprehensive planning for the aging now beginning to occur at the regional level. Following is a discussion of major findings from the study and resources for assisting older people in meeting some of their more pressing needs.

Housing

Older Guilfordians apparently valued the security of home ownership as observed through the large percentage living in their own homes and infrequent changes in residence. When moving had occurred during the past five years, relocation was usually within the county. Strong ties to neighborhood or to local children or other persons were reflected in the length of time that most older people had remained in the same locality. There was considerable evidence that most older persons expected, or at least hoped, to remain indefinitely in their homes, near, but independent of relatives. Numbers of the aging had not given thought to alternate forms of living arrangements in the event that they became necessary. Housing costs, especially home maintenance, was listed as a major problem by the one-fourth of older people who reported that their incomes were inadequate. The importance of older people remaining in their own homes has been recognized and many efforts are being made at the national level to make this option available.

The 1971 White House Conference on Aging recommended that four methods for enabling older people to remain in their homes be explored:

1. Ways or mechanisms to enable persons to voluntarily utilize the equities in their homes

2. Ways to increase older people's discretionary income while remaining in their homes

3. Programs to preserve and repair physical housing structure

4. Property tax relief.

Very little progress has been made on these specific recommendations. The Homestead Act in North Carolina allows eligible older homeowners a $5,000 deduction on their homes for tax purposes. This legislation has had rather low visibility among older citizens and eligibility is restricted to a small segment of the population.

Aside from the financial aspects, living arrangements in later life must also be geared to the individual's health and physical mobility. The 1971 White House Conference also recommended the development of four categories of residentially oriented settings which relate to the different service requirements of older people:

1. Long-term care facilities for the sick

2. Facilities with limited medical, food, and homemaker services

3. Congregate housing which would provide food and personal services but not medical services

4. Housing for wholly independent living with recreation and activity programs.

Administrative action has occurred as a result of the preceding housing recommendations. Several important measures have evolved under the Department of Housing and Urban Development (HUD). These developments include the establishment of the position of Assistant to the Secretary for Programs for the Elderly and the Handicapped, increased efforts to improve security in public housing projects, and experiments to evaluate a program of housing allowances for low and moderate income families. This last measure allows freedom to recipients to use allotments for renting a house or an apartment anywhere they choose. Other significant action as a result of the 1971 White House Conference has been a vigorous implementation of an eight-point program requested by the president for upgrading nursing homes. The federal government now assumes full responsibility for the costs of inspection of Medicare nursing homes and intermediate care facilities under Medicaid.

Findings from a recent national housing study, under the direction of the President's Counsellor for Community Development, will form the basis for future presidential recommendations in the field of housing. Data from this project will contribute to the development of policies that will help assure that older people have greater access to adequate housing within their means and best suited to their needs. These new housing policies will be reflected in the president's Better Communities Act, legislation which provides revenue sharing for community development.

Also to be explored as a result of findings from the national housing study are the problems of special groups of older people which include low income and minority groups. In the Guilford study, problems of income and general unhappiness were more severe among some older people than among others, in particular, to rural black females, low socioeconomic groups, and widows. Other housing considerations as a result of the national housing study will include:

1. The insurance of adequate replacement units before older persons are displaced by federally assisted projects

2. Support for the use of model project funds by the Administration on Aging and HUD for demonstration home maintenance programs

3. Development of policies in the area of long-term care, quality of institutional care, and alternatives to institutional care.

One of the more traditional alternatives to housing for the aging is also under current consideration--the extended family concept. Efforts are being made to foster federal legislation that would make available more financial incentives to families providing housing and related care in their own homes for their relatives. Such incentives would be in the form of more substantial tax deductions. In the Guilford study, approximately one in every three older persons lived with a family member, other than a spouse. In some cases, however, arrangements were designed for the support or maintenance of younger family members in the home and were at the expense of the older family member.

Employment

Approximately 80 percent of the Guilford sample was fully retired. A moderate amount of dissatisfaction with retirement was observed, mainly attributable to the loss of old work patterns rather than to the loss of income. Poor health, however, was the major reason given for retirement. The few older people who continued to work (7.3 percent) enjoyed their work very much and generally had no future plans to retire.

There appeared to be little desire among retired persons for re-employment. Three reasons for low interest in re-employment, aside from health, possibly existed among older people in Guilford County. Former job types at age 50 had been generally in the skilled and unskilled occupational categories. Many of these work types are age related--they demand considerable strength, dexterity, and speed. Recognizing age related losses in these areas, retired workers probably did not see themselves as able to compete or function adequately in former occupations. Many women, particularly housewives or widows, had no previous occupational skills or experiences to which to return. Due to mechanization, some former job types of a few years ago no longer exist. Also, there has been considerable age discrimination in employment methods within recent years. These and other reasons may have discouraged older people from attempting to reenter the labor market.

National efforts are now being made to increase employment opportunities for older Americans. A directive has been sent by the president to heads of all federal departments and agencies stating that age be no barrier to federal positions for which an individual is otherwise qualified. Furthermore, the president has directed the Department of Labor to work with the Public Employment Service to open job opportunities in both public and private sectors, including part-time work, for persons 65 years and over. Another significant effort in the creation of job opportunities occurred in 1973 with the doubling of funds for the manpower project for older workers.

A recent major liberalization in the Retirement Test might encourage more older persons into the part-time labor force. A beneficiary (Social Security) can now earn up to $2,400 yearly without penalty and with less than previous forfeits for earnings over $2,400. Another incentive to older people for seeking employment is a new provision in Social Security, the delayed retired credit, which provides for increments in a worker's old age benefits by 1 percent for each year after 1970 for which the worker between 65-75 did not receive benefits because of earnings from work.

Income

The median annual income of $2,300 observed for older Guilfordians was considerably below the minimum standard of income adequacy of the intermediate budget for single persons ($3,375) established by the Bureau of Labor Statistics in 1970. Model budgets established by the Bureau are used in national policy decisions. One of the three budget levels, the intermediate level of $4,500 for a couple in the spring of 1970, was recommended by the 1971 White House Conference to serve as the standard of income adequacy for future policy making--with the stipulation that it receive annual adjustment. A lower level budget has been the usual model accepted for policy making. An interagency task force of the Human Resources Committee of the Domestic Council has been established to come to grips with developing a definition of "adequate" income for older persons.

Social Security benefits were the major source of income

reported by the Guilford sample. Increases totalling more than 60 percent have occurred between 1969 through the spring of 1974. A number of other actions in the direction of assuring an adequate income for the aging have been initiated as a result of recommendations from delegates to the 1971 White House Conference. Widows and widowers aged 65 years or older are now entitled to 100 percent of the benefits that were paid to their deceased spouse. This change is very significant since, nationally, 58 percent of the population aged 65 and older are women, most of whom depend primarily on the Social Security benefits earned by their husbands. Previously, widows were eligible for only 82.5 percent of the amount of deceased husbands' benefits. Considerable poverty has been found among older women, and in particular, widows. In the Guilford study, widows expressed significantly more unhappiness in life than married women. This unhappiness might have been due to inadequate income although many variables other than income could also have contributed to unhappiness in later life.

A recent piece of federal legislation is thought by some to be the most significant in the income area since the 1935 Social Security Act. The plan forms a "financial floor" under the income of the aging. The legislation replaced the Old Age Assistance Program with a federally financed program of supplemental security income which guarantees minimum monthly income of $140 per individual and $210 monthly for couples. It is estimated that this program will benefit an estimated 4.6 million older people, or one-fourth of Americans 65 years and older. As previously stated, one-fourth of older people in the Guilford sample reported their incomes inadequate in meeting their needs.

In the Guilford study, an inadequate income was reported more frequently by blacks than by whites and by older people from low socioeconomic backgrounds. Unhappiness in life was also observed more frequently among blacks and persons from a low social position as well as by persons living in areas outside of the two cities. Delegates to the White House Conference pointed out that income needs exceed all other priorities with the black aged and recommended establishing a system that would provide at least a guaranteed, moderate income for all black aged.

The needs and problems of rural older people have also been recognized at the national level. One-third of older Americans living in areas outside of the central cities and suburban areas live in poverty. Retirement income is lower in rural areas because few workers were covered by private pension plans. Most rural people became eligible for Social Security relatively recently and have had fewer years of covered earnings and thus their benefits are low. Chronic ill health, a devastating blow to income, is also more prevalent among older rural people than among urban people. Although Guilford County is classified as a Standard Metropolitan Statistical Area, older people living outside the corporate limits of the two cities displayed many characteristics of a rural population. Results of life styles set down during earlier periods before the "metropolitan era" were evidenced through low incomes and educational levels and less satisfaction in life.

Several other changes in the Social Security Program are discussed in other sections of this chapter. It should be pointed out that although action has been taken on numerous White House Conference recommendations for assuring adequate incomes for the aging, most actions fall short of the original recommendations and actual needs of the older population.

Health

Health was reported as the number one problem by older people in Guilford County. There was some awareness on the part of older people of the value of preventive health care. Despite the prevalence of multiple chronic ailments, a large number of people reported having gone to a physician during the previous year for routine check-ups rather than for illness. It must be acknowledged, however, that approximately one-third of the older people interviewed also stated that during the previous year they had either just "lived with their physical problems" or they had prescribed their own medication.

The annual health cost per respondent was $368.83--considerably below the 1970 national figure reported for older people. Supplemental sources of medical payments through private insurance plans, Medicare, Medicaid, relatives, and Old Age Assistance were not reflected in the sample's medical costs and contributed to the underestimate. Nevertheless, almost one-half of the sample indicated that they had personally assumed all of their medical costs during the previous year.

There can be no income security, or personal security, so long as heavy and unpredictable health costs threaten incomes of the aging. Despite new health programs resulting from the Older American Act of 1965, many gaps in medical services exist. Gaps in services were prime targets at the 1971 White House Conference. Recent administrative concern for comprehensive health care for all Americans has prompted new concepts of health care.

One of the most significant and promising concepts of care, the Health Maintainance Organization (HMO), is now under development at the request of the president. The HMO concept is planned to enable citizens to obtain quality health care at reasonable cost regardless of income. The new program will bring into a single organization the physician, the hospital, and the clinic in order to provide comprehensive health service in an efficient manner in a wide range of settings. Payment for these comprehensive services will be on a monthly flat-rate basis through a national insurance program.

A national health insurance plan will be submitted to the 94th Congress. If the plan corresponds to proposed legislation, participation will be mandatory and costs to individuals will vary according to assessment of monthly or yearly income of beneficiaries. Coverage under the propsed plan is expected to be extensive, including all health needs of the individual from major surgery to dental work, hospital, nursing home, and out-patient care. The distinct advantages of the proposed insurance and health care plans are the ease of access to appropriate specialists and removal of medical expenses from the "unknown" category. Because of the chronic nature of many health problems of the aging, the revived clinic concept in health services would be of considerable value. Clinics are efficient as dispensers of continuing medical care for out-patients.

Legislative action has recently been taken which limits future increases in the premium for supplementary medical insurance under the Medicare program. This same legislation broadened the extent of past hospital care available to older persons under Medicare and relieves beneficiaries from liability in certain situations in which Medicare claims are disallowed and the beneficiary is without fault.

Transportation

A discussion of the needs of the aging is incomplete without the consideration of transportation. No system of services regardless of how innovative or comprehensive is accessible to the majority of older people unless transportation is also a component of the system. In Guilford County, more than half the older people surveyed reported that they were dependent upon others for transportation. The cost, operation, and upkeep on an automobile is beyond the income of many older persons. The present inflation of gasoline prices only serves to compound this problem. Poor health, slower reaction time, and biases of insurance companies toward older drivers further complicate the operation of a car. The paucity or inefficiency of public transportation in rural and urban areas also decreases the mobility of older people.

A number of measures have been taken to assist older Americans with transportation problems. Only a few actions will be mentioned here. The president has directed that all federal grants which provide services for older persons also insure the transportation needed by the recipients of the programs. The president has also proposed that states and localities expand resources in the mass transportation area through the use of funds now in the Highway Trust Fund. The administration has endorsed no-fault insurance and has encouraged the use of school buses to transport older people to needed programs and services. Some legislative action to improve transportation for the elderly has occurred in several states. Examples of these actions include: (1) reduced fare or fare-free systems for public transportation; (2) the use of school buses, mini buses, and government passenger vehicles to transport older people; (3) protection against discrimination in auto licensing; and (4) compensation to volunteer drivers for the elderly.

Transportation resources, no matter how broad the range available, will not benefit older people unless coordinated, comprehensive systems are developed within and between towns, cities, and outlying areas. Existing transportation should be coordinated with publicly funded programs and more individualized, flexible transportation should be developed to meet the broad spectrum of transportation needs of older people.

Implications for Regional Planning

As the nation moves in the direction of comprehensive programs in health, housing, income maintenance, transportation, and education for all Americans, effective regional planning will become more and more imperative. The challenge to regional planners for the aging will be to search out local needs and resources for older people and to design appropriate systems of services. Data from the Guilford study showed that problems associated with health, income, and happiness were not the same for blacks and whites, men and women, and different social groups. Data also showed that within a rather small geographical area, which is assumedly metropolitan in character, urban services did not reach all older people outside of the two cities.

North Carolina, as well as other states, is currently moving in the direction of regional planning for all citizens through the organization of its 17 multicounty planning regional units. Amendments in the Older American Act have made funds available for the creation and implementation of area plans to meet the needs of the aging. The type and extent of plans for each county within the given region will vary according to the elderly's needs.

Regional or area planning has been further enhanced through other recent legislation. Federal monies may now be used under General Revenue Sharing by both state and local governments if they choose to support coordinated and comprehensive service programs for older people. Examples of possible programs are numerous and they include: (1) health services through health maintenance organizations; (2) homemaker-homeaide services; (3) mental health services for the physically and mentally handicapped; (4) services in the areas of education, transportation, law, housing, nutrition, and home repairs; (5) home visitation and telephone reassurance services; (6) operation of senior centers; (7) counseling, training, and placement programs for those interested in employment or in participating as volunteers in community service activities; and (8) information and referral services.

The horizon is very bright in terms of current national, state, and local interest in meeting the needs of the increasing numbers of older people. Opportunities for helping to fill later years with the security of improved health, income, and life satisfaction appear limitless. Comprehensive and efficient planning within a geographical area will piece together and strengthen existing systems and supplement or create other services where needed. Fragmentation and duplication of services (where inefficient) will be abolished in the process.

Older people within a given geographical area may display a diversity of attitudes toward systems designed for them. Many persons for whom programs are intended have been very self-reliant for many years. Older people may refuse available programs of services because they are unskilled in taking the initiative in dealing with "government officials." Planning for the diversity of older people found within a region must be devised in ways which are not threatening to the dignity or foreign to the elderly within the multiplanning unit. More importantly, regional planning must involve the beneficiaries as well as the implementors of plans--the aging and program sponsors.

NOTES

1. The study used as the basis for this paper was Agricultural Experiment Station Project 3240, The Aged in North Carolina: Physical, Social, and Environmental Characteristics and Sources of Assistance. The survey was a joint effort of the School of Home Economics of The University of North Carolina at Greensboro; the Agricultural Experiment Station, North Carolina State University, Raleigh; and the Cooperative States Research Service, United States Department of Agriculture, Washington, D.C.

2. For purposes of this study, all areas in the county falling outside the Greensboro and High Point city limits were classified as rural.

3. The data used in this chapter reflect only a portion of the findings. Complete findings are forthcoming in an Agricultural Experiment Station Technical Bulletin from North Carolina State University at Raleigh.

4. This figure is probably underestimated because of the difficulty in recall encountered by the subjects when asked about medical costs they had incurred during the previous year. In 1970, the national figure on annual medical costs per person 65 years and older was nearly $600.

REFERENCES

Advanced Planning Section, Guilford County Planning Department
(1973) "Percents and Distributions of the Population
(Guilford County) by Decade." Mimeographed. Greensboro,
N.C.: Advanced Planning Section, Guilford County Planning
Department.

Hollingshead, A. B. (1965) *Two Factor Index of Social Position*.
New Haven, Conn.: A. B. Hollingshead.

Kivett, Vira R.; Bishop, Cynthia L.; and Watson, James A. (1973)
"Characteristics and Needs of Persons 65 Years and Older in
Guilford County, North Carolina." Technical Report 6.
Greensboro: Home Economics Center for Research, The University of North Carolina at Greensboro.

U.S. Bureau of the Census (1970) *Census of Population and Housing, 1970*. Census Tracts, Final Report PHC(1)-83. Washington: U.S. Government Printing Office.

U.S. Congress. Senate. Committee on Labor and Public Welfare.
Subcommittee on Aging. (1973a) *Post-White House Conference on Aging Reports. Toward a New Attitude on Aging*. Washington: U.S. Government Printing Office.

_____ (1973b) *Towards a National Policy on Aging: Proceedings of the 1971 White House Conference on Aging*. Vol. 2.
Washington: U.S. Government Printing Office.

10

Varied Perspectives on Crowding

VINCENT M. LOLORDO

Interest in the effects of high population density on the physiology, behavior, and survival of groups of animals and men is now widespread. Much of the current research on the effects of high population density seems to be motivated by concern for the human condition, specifically that, since many parts of the world are already "overcrowded" and still experiencing rapid population growth, only understanding the effects of high population density will give us a chance to prevent disaster. If we accept this perspective, then what questions should we be asking?

The obvious question is: What are the effects of high population density upon behaviors that we would agree are important--physiological responses, cognitive functioning, social behaviors, including aggressive, sexual, and maternal behaviors, and other behaviors which affect the maintenance of the social order?

Second, if high density does have substantial, undesirable effects, how does it produce these effects? Answers to this question might refer to the total amount of stimulation from the environment, to an increased number of social interactions, or to some combination of these and many other factors. To answer the question satisfactorily, we need to know what variables, including nonspatial variables, facilitate or reduce the undesirable consequences of high-density situations (Stokols 1973). As such

---

I would like to thank Andrew Baker and Donald Foree for their comments on an earlier draft of this chapter.

information accumulates, we may begin to understand the psychological mechanisms by which high population density produces its effects.

Third, how can we design the environment to mitigate any noxious consequences of high population density? A comprehensive answer to this question obviously depends upon the answers to the first two questions, although the collection of just a small amount of "clean" data bearing on the fundamental questions will very likely permit some progress in design.

At the present time, answers to these questions are tentative at best. In what follows I shall review very selectively research on the effects of high population density, and present the sorts of answers that have been suggested by this research. My bias is that of an experimental psychologist who studies the behavior of dogs, rats, and pigeons.

RESEARCH WITH LOWER ANIMALS

The first research area that bears on the questions raised earlier is the study of the effects of high population density on the physiology, behavior, and survival of animal populations. In fact, several different traditions, each with its own methodology and focus, are represented in this research. The investigations vary in their use of confined or free-roaming populations, in the extent to which the subject populations are susceptible to extrinsic checks on population growth--for example, food shortages, predation, and disease--and in their focus on physiological, behavioral, or demographic outcomes.

The classic study of the effects of high population density on the behavior of confined animal populations was performed by J. B. Calhoun (1962, 1971), who conducted a series of long-term studies of confined populations of albino rats. In a given replication of the experiment, from 32-56 rats, equally divided between males and females, were placed in an enclosure consisting of four equal-sized pens, each containing food, a water fountain, and an elevated burrow with four nest boxes. The pens were functionally in a row, with ramps permitting movement from one pen to the next. By the twelfth month the populations had grown, and each comprised 80 adults. Thereafter infants which survived weaning were removed to hold the number constant.

When the first group of male rats reached maturity, they began to engage in the normal round-robin of fights, which eventually established relative dominance. In the end pens, since there was only one entrance, it became possible for one dominant male to take over the area as his territory. The dominant male established his control over the pen and the females which lived therein by engaging subordinate males in fights as they tried to come down the ramp into the pen. After several defeats the subordinates would no longer even attempt to enter the end pens. The social environments in these pens appeared to be normal.

The situation was quite different in the middle pens, which could be entered from either side. A single male never established dominance in these pens, and they became crowded with rats, including most of the males in the enclosure. In the crowded middle pens there developed what Calhoun called a "behavioral sink." The pellet food provided for the rats took some time to eat, so that a rat wandering through the pens was very likely to encounter another rat at the feeder, and would himself stop and eat. Gradually, there developed a tendency to eat only when other rats were eating, producing a large gathering of rats at the feeders in the middle pens. Thus rats in these pens were required to adjust to a greatly increased number of social contacts per day.

Such an adjustment did not occur; rather a variety of severe social pathologies affecting both males and females developed. Sustained, integrated activities necessary for the survival of the population were disrupted by the too frequent encounters among rats. Females built progressively less adequate nests, and other maternal behaviors also disintegrated, resulting in an infant mortality rate of 90 percent in the middle pens. Several deviant classes of male rats developed. Even the least deviant males became pathologically aggressive at times, attacking females and juveniles. Such attacks rarely occur under normal circumstances. Other deviant classes of males included passive creatures which withdrew from social interactions almost completely, and extremely active, hypersexual beasts called "probers" by Calhoun. The probers were abnormally relentless in their pursuit of estrous females, even pursuing them into the normally sacrosanct burrow.

Abnormally high maternal mortality rates from disorders of pregnancy and parturition occurred in the middle pens. Calhoun (1962) maintained that, in time, failures of reproduction would have led to extinction of the colony. He removed the four healthiest male and female rats from the middle pens when the experiment was terminated after 16 months, and placed them together in a low density environment. They produced fewer than the expected number of offspring, and none of those survived to maturity. Other observers have also noted that young born during periods of high population density are less fit (Davis 1971).

Thus exposure to high population density can produce disruption of the normal social order, with disastrous consequences for the colony, when confinement prevents dispersal in response to increasingly aversive conditions. Further, it has been demonstrated that rats confined for several months under conditions of high population density learn complex tasks less well than those exposed to moderate density (Goeckner, Greenough, and Mead 1973). Results qualitatively similar to, though different in detail from, Calhoun's have been obtained when populations of other species, including mice (Calhoun 1971) and rabbits (Myers et al. 1971), were placed in a laboratory situation under conditions of high population density. Southwick (1966) found that halving the area available to a captive group of rhesus monkeys markedly increases the number of aggressive interactions among members of the group.

Dispersal

One obvious question posed by studies using confined animals is: Would the consequences be the same if dispersal were permitted? To answer this question we turn to research from somewhat more natural settings. An ethologist, Wynne-Edwards (1965), argued that dispersal is the most critical factor in the natural regulation of animal numbers. He maintained that social institutions in the animal world--territoriality and dominance hierarchies--have the function of forcing surplus animals, usually young or subordinates, to disperse, thereby preventing overgrazing and destruction of the habitat. Territorial plumage, scent marking, greetings, songs, et cetera, serve to inform an animal of the intensity of the competition, and thus to affect the likelihood of his leaving the area. For Wynne-Edwards, population regulation is due to a sensitive intrinsic homeostatic mechanism which operates efficiently in all but the unstable environments of desert and polar regions, and on agricultural land, where populations fluctuate more widely. From this perspective the space limitations imposed on Calhoun's rats prevented dispersal from the middle pens, and thus disrupted the normal machinery of homeostasis. Disaster followed, in the form of mechanisms alternative to dispersal.

C. J. Krebs and his colleagues (1973) have done very interesting research on dispersal as a reaction to high population density, chiefly on small rodents whose natural populations fluctuate widely in two- or three-year cycles. These cycles have a phase of rapid increase, a peak phase in which density is high and constant, and a decline phase. The birth rate is markedly reduced during peak and decline phases, principally because of a shortening in the breeding season. At the peak, the death rate of small juveniles increases dramatically, and as the decline ensues, the death rate of adults also increases.

Krebs et al. (1973) attempted to understand how these demographic changes came about by comparing populations of voles confined to a two-acre field with unconfined populations in a similar area. Both populations increased in size, but the two diverged sharply during the early peak phase, with the confined population reaching a density three times as high as the control population. The overpopulation of the confined voles led to overgrazing and habitat destruction, producing a sharp decline in population, due in part to starvation. Thus confining the population markedly reduced the effectiveness of the homeostatic machinery, thereby implicating dispersal as a very critical mechanism.

By means of trapping, Krebs et al. determined that dispersal was most common in the increase phase of an unconfined population, and least common in the decline phase, when most of the losses must have been deaths in situ. Since dispersal in large numbers occurred in the increase phase, Krebs et al. argued that dispersal was not a direct response to a large absolute density, but that the quality of the dispersers must somehow be important. Perhaps the dispersers are animals which are sensitive to rapid increases in density, but would not exhibit sensitivity to high density in other ways, for example, their fertility would not be limited as a response to high density. Hence fencing keeps these beasts in the population and there is continued rapid growth. Then only when the population is very large do other intrinsic mechanisms like those Calhoun observed, plus extrinsic checks, take their toll.

Although the research of Krebs et al. indicates the importance of dispersal in the natural regulation of animal populations, Calhoun's data indicate that dispersal is not the only intrinsic mechanism of population regulation. There has been considerable research on behavioral-endocrine mechanisms that may work in concert with, or as alternatives to, dispersal or social pathology in regulating numbers. The relative importance of the diverse mechanisms varies across species (Christian 1971).

Physiology of Crowding

I shall review our knowledge of the physiology of crowding very generally, for it is an esoteric and very complex area. Briefly, diverse forms of stress, including that produced by high population density, result in marked physiological effects in lower animals. It is well known that the increase in the number of social interactions that accompanies overcrowding tends to overload the adrenals. This effect, which can be detected by greater than normal adrenal weights, results in a complex of reactions, including retardation of maturation, reduced fertility, a high rate of intrauterine mortality, inadequate lactation, and decreased resistance to disease or other added stress

(Christian and Davis 1964). Furthermore, species which have periodic population eruptions differ from those which do not in the sensitivity to population density of the behavioral-endocrine mechanisms which inhibit reproduction (Christian 1971).

The critical mediator between increased population density and the stress reactions listed above is the increased number of social interactions any individual must experience. Although animal studies of high population density whose prime focus is behavioral are relatively rare, recently it has been shown that increases in population density are directly related to increases in agonistic behavior.

For example, Gregor et al. (1972) confined different sized groups of deermice in cages of a given size, thereby producing conditions of either moderate or high population density. Crowded animals engaged in more contact behavior per animal, such as mutual grooming, than did uncrowded animals. Further, there were many more occurrences of agonistic behavior--threats, attack, and defensive behaviors--among crowded than among uncrowded animals. Barash (1974) has observed a strong positive correlation between the number of individuals in an Olympic marmot colony in the spring, the number of greeting ceremonies performed by each individual, and the likelihood that two-year-old marmots will leave the colony. Myers et al. (1971) noted marked increases in the aggressive behavior of rabbits as a function of increased density, when initial group size was held constant, and available area varied across groups.

The development of the adrenal responses may be produced by brief, infrequent agonistic encounters, provided that these encounters are intense. For example, as few as two one-minute exposures to a trained fighter mouse per day for seven days produced a 14 percent increase in adrenal weights in mice (Bronson and Eleftheriou 1964). However, Christian (1963) has shown that fighting or wounding per se are not necessary conditions of the adrenal response to increased density. Thus there seems to be a trade-off between the intensity and frequency of interactions in this regard, such that many confrontations which fail to lead to actual fights will have an effect comparable to that of a few fights. The impact of these confrontations on the physiology of a given animal is a function of his social rank. The dominant animal's physiology is least affected by increased density, while low-ranking animals, including young adult males, may be most affected (Davis 1971).

The displays and "conventional competitions" cited by Wynne-Edwards (1965) may lead to marked physiological changes in subordinate animals, or cause them to disperse, responses tending to limit the size of the population. One focus of further research in this area should be the relations among dispersal, "social pathology" and the other behavioral-endocrine responses to density within the same population. Such studies would provide a more integrated view of population regulation.

Applications of Animal Research to Humans

Can we apply the information we have obtained from research on lower animals to the human species? To begin with an obvious point, studies on animals cannot tell us whether human populations are susceptible to the intrinsic mechanisms of population regulation we have discussed. Wynne-Edwards (1965) argued that behavioral mechanisms of population regulation in the form of traditional customs and taboos existed in groups of primitive men, but became unnecessary with the rise of technology, and, unfortunately, have disappeared. Indeed, the recent history of some densely populated cities in less developed countries suggests that the birth rate may remain high until extrinsic checks on growth, notably food shortage, begin to exert a terrible control over behavior.

On the other hand, Olin (1966) noted that in chronically crowded conditions, humans often display behaviors parallel to those of Calhoun's rats: (1) sexual hyperactivity, (2) neglect and maltreatment of children, and (3) criminality in general. Schorr (1963:31-32) maintained that overcrowding had the following effects on people:

> A perception of one's self that leads to pessimism and passivity, stress to which the individual cannot adapt, poor health, and a state of dissatisfaction; pleasure in company but not in solitude, cynicism about people and organizations, a high degree of sexual stimulation without legitimate outlet, and difficulty in household management and child rearing . . .

Olin (1966) also argued that with urbanization has come an increase in the extent of excess male (to female) mortality, perhaps testifying to an increase in stress produced by increased social competition. Despite these provocative parallels with the behavior of animals, it is not obvious that sensitive intrinsic mechanisms of population regulation exist in humans. Further, the existence of such mechanisms would by no means guarantee a rosy future for mankind, since many of the mechanisms observed by Calhoun are rather unpleasant.

In any case, it is clear that humans are sensitive to various stressors (Friedman and Ader 1968). Thus, short of regulating our numbers, we may still expect to suffer some of the noxious effects of the behavioral-endocrine mechanism, for example, increased aggressiveness in response to high and increasing population densities, especially if dispersal is not a real possibility. In many cases it will not be: Consider the plight of the inhabitants of a crowded city in an already crowded country like India, or even of the very poor in the ghetto.

Effects of High Density

Regarding our second question, we know much less about the way in which density exerts its effects upon animals than we know about the effects themselves, perhaps because the focus of most of the animal research has been on the physiological and demographic consequences of high population density, rather than on behavior. Obviously increased density has its effects through an increased number of social interactions among animals. In some cases an increased number of contacts among animals might also result from increased group size, even with density held constant. An increased number of interactions might produce negative effects in several ways.

1. Too frequent social contacts might repeatedly disrupt goal-directed sequences of behavior, such as the nest building of Calhoun's rats. Such interruptions might themselves cause aggressive behavior directed at the intruder, as well as an increased state of arousal which would feed back into the system, contributing to increased activity and more contacts.

2. An increase in the number of animals which are interacting prolongs the social familiarization process, making the formation of stable social groups more difficult.

3. If many of the increased interactions forced upon an animal by a situation of high population density can be conceptualized as uncontrollable aversive events, then by analogy with the research on the effects of inescapable shock (Maier, Seligman, and Solomon 1969), one might expect extreme passivity to characterize at least some of the animals in a population at high density (Goeckner, Greenough, and Mead 1973). Calhoun and others have noted that such creatures do exist, but we do not know why only some members of a given population respond to high density in this way.

In any case, the animal research should concentrate on obtaining behavioral data which would permit evaluation of these and the many other possible behavioral mechanisms of the response to high population density.

RESEARCH WITH PEOPLE

There have been three distinct kinds of research on humans which bear upon the effects of high population density. First, there have been surveys assessing the diverse effects of high density in a natural setting, for example, by correlating density and various social pathologies across parts of a city. Second, there have recently appeared some reports of experiments on the effects of a few hours' exposure to very high population densities on task performance and social behaviors. Third, over the last 15 years considerable interest has developed in the human use of space (Hall 1966; Sommer 1969). I shall consider aspects of each of these varieties of research.

Density in a Natural Setting

In the most recent, and methodologically soundest, of the correlational studies of the effects of density upon human behavior, Galle, Gove, and McPherson (1972) correlated five indices of social pathology with several indices of population density across 75 community areas in Chicago. In addition they developed measures of social class and ethnicity, which were calculated for each area. Their objective was to determine the extent to which population density contributed to social pathology, even after social class and ethnicity had been taken into account--to isolate the effect of density.

Using the number of persons per acre as the measure of density, Galle, Gove, and McPherson found that when social class and ethnicity were controlled statistically, partial correlations of density with indices of (1) fertility; (2) mortality; (3) ineffectual care of the young; (4) asocial, aggressive behavior; and (5) psychiatric disorder were essentially zero. That is, there was no real relation between the number of persons per acre and social pathology.

Undaunted, Galle and his colleagues sought a new measure of density that would reflect more directly the likelihood that the environment would force excess social contacts upon an individual. They came up with two such measures, the number of persons per room and the number of rooms per housing unit. They also looked at structural measures of density, the number of housing units per structure and the number of structures per acre. Additional correlational analyses using these new components of total density revealed that the number of persons per room was an important contributor to the level of social pathology. It was directly related to the levels of mortality, fertility, ineffectual parental care, and juvenile delinquency. The number of rooms per housing unit was the measure of density most strongly (though inversely) related to the level of admission to mental hospitals.

Galle, Gove, and McPherson noted that with an increase in the number of persons per room should come an increasing number of social obligations, progressive limitations on individual freedom, and perhaps sensory overload. These pressures might well produce irritability and withdrawal, which in turn would affect the level of social pathology. For example, when a child leaves the overcrowded apartment, both parents and children would be reinforced by a reduction in the level of irritations. Thus leaving the apartment would tend to become the typical response to aversive circumstances, perhaps setting the stage for a higher level of juvenile delinquency than in a district containing less crowded apartments.

It is worth pointing out that the correlation between the number of persons per room and fertility was positive in Chicago, while fertility declines with increasing density in lower animals. Galle and his colleagues proposed several testable explanations of this discrepancy, though the tests await data on the relation between the number of persons per room and: (1) the frequency of sexual intercourse; (2) the likelihood that birth control measures will be used. The last datum would be especially interesting, since the authors speculated that continually being forced to react to others might disrupt a predisposition to formulate and carry out long-range plans, including family planning.

Finally, the Galle research suggested that the number of rooms per dwelling unit might be inversely related to the level of admissions to mental hospitals because people who have extreme difficulties in getting along with others seek small apartments where they live alone.

To sum up, the provocative research of Galle, Gove, and McPherson illustrates a general point: that the "best" measure of density may well be situation-dependent (Zlutnick and Altman 1972). Further, it provides a mine of hypotheses about the effects of density on human behaviors and survival, though the authors recognized that it cannot demonstrate any causal relations nor elucidate the dynamic interactions among variables at an individual level.

Density in a Brief Encounter

Experiments on the effects of high population density on human behavior are a relatively recent development. They tend to be predicated on the assumption that the effect of high density is proportional to the duration of exposure to that density, so that if long-term exposure to high density has important effects, then a brief exposure to a very high density should have discernible effects.

Freedman, Klevansky, and Ehrlich (1971) sought effects of four-hour exposures to very high density, on the assumption that such density would be an aversive stimulus. In their experiments the subjects, high school students or women aged 25-60 years, were strangers to each other. They were expected to sit in one place during the experiment, and were never required to move around. In the first series of studies, which placed as many as nine people in an area of 35 square feet, no effects attributable to density were found on a variety of tasks, whether interesting or dull, group or individual, brief or lengthy enough to be boring, under a variety of motivational conditions. Freedman and his colleagues tentatively concluded that high density per se is not an aversive stimulus in the usual sense, that it does not increase drive or arousal, and that it does not affect performance negatively.

In short, high density is not inherently evil. From the perspective of the research on animals, this outcome is not surprising. In Calhoun's and the other studies cited in the first part of this chapter, the animals tended to move around in the available space, engaging in goal-directed behavior. Under conditions of high density they got in each other's way. None of these things happened in the procedure used by Freedman, Klevansky, and Ehrlich, and there was no effect of density.

Perceptions of Needed and Available Space

The point concerning the lack of effect from density may be clarified by considering the distinction between high density and crowding proposed by Stokols (1972). He suggested that the physical condition of high density is very likely a necessary but not a sufficient condition for the feeling of being crowded. The potential inconvenience produced by high density would lead to perceived inconvenience only under certain circumstances, for example, when the task required coordinated movement of people, when competition with others was involved, or when the people had little prior experience with high density. The presence of such factors would, according to Stokols, lead to a perception of the disparity between needed and available space, creating a motivational state which could only be reduced if the disparity were eliminated, such as by leaving the crowded situation or modifying standards of spatial adequacy. Unsuccessful attempts to reduce the perceived disparity would, in this model, produce behaviors symptomatic of stress--heightened aggressiveness and physiological effects. In the terms of Stokols' model, the situation used by Freedman and colleagues would not have produced the disparity between needed and available space, and thus density would not have been expected to affect performance.

Several experiments have included conditions which might be expected to produce a perceived disparity between needed and available space. Some of the outcomes of these studies suggest that mildly negative effects upon social behaviors may be produced by brief exposures to high density. These effects have often taken the form of interactions between density and sex. For example, the members of an all-male group in a small room made more competitive choices in a modified prisoner's dilemma game (which permits either competitive or cooperative choices) than did men in a large room, while the reverse effect held for women in all-female groups (Freedman et al. 1972).

The same interaction was observed in another situation designed to arouse and measure aggressiveness, the mock jury situation. Women in a small "courtroom" gave lesser sentences to defendants accused of violent crimes than did women in a larger room; but men were more severe in the small room (Freedman et al. 1972). The reported liking for other jury members showed the same interaction, as did the amount of facial regard of other members of a group during a 20-minute discussion of some choice-dilemmas about which a unanimous decision had to be reached (Ross et al. 1973).

The Ross et al. study is notable in obtaining independent evidence that the size of the room did affect the perception of crowding, as measured by verbal reports. Ross et al. suggested that males apparently found the interpersonal distance in the small room too close, while females found the interpersonal distance in the large room too great. In this regard, Sommer (1969) has shown that females choose to sit closer to other females than males do to other males. These outcomes may reflect differences in the socialization process for males and females in our culture, the male role requiring independence and the maintenance of psychological distance from other males, while the female role requires dependence and intimacy with other females (Liebman 1970).

EVALUATING THE STUDIES

It is perhaps too early to assess the contributions of these experimental studies. The observed effects do not seem impressively large, but such a statement assumes that density really has big effects on human behavior. Further, by their very nature such studies cannot produce the dramatic effects that have been obtained in long-term studies of captive animals, or have been extracted from naturalistic observations of life in a crowded city.

As short-term studies, and furthermore studies which vary density across conditions rather than longitudinally, the experiments on people lack an aspect of the animal studies which seems important. In the latter, changes in the population density, by altering the number of interactions among animals, in time alter the kinds of interactions as well, for example, they become interactions among stressed rather than nonstressed animals. Nonetheless, the human experimental work on crowding is in its infancy, and the possibility of methodological advances which will result in more robust effects should not be dismissed. Further, the analytic nature of experimental research makes it best suited for the study of the sorts of human interactions which will interact with density to produce the perception of crowding and possible concomitant negative effects.

Returning to our original questions, we find a great many suggested answers to the first question--concerning the important effects of high density on behavior--from both animal and human studies, though more research should be done on the effects of density on problem solving. Further, we find the answers from the animal studies and those from correlational studies of some human populations often surprisingly similar, though there are discrepancies, and there will certainly be marked differences among human cultures in the response to high density. For example, Draper (1973) noted that the !Kung bushmen of southwest Africa live in villages where the population density is extremely high, yet seem not to be stressed. Draper suggested that the absence of stress might be due to the acceptable option of moving from one village to another, or to the absence of strangers within miles of the village. In any case, cross-cultural analyses may suggest a variety of hypotheses about variables which modulate the effects of density.

There has been much speculation about the mechanism by which high density has its effects, but very few behavioral data of the sort which would permit theory-testing have been obtained even from animal research, where important effects of density have been observed. By providing such data, particularly from multivariate studies which include several behavioral and physiological dependent variables, research with both animals and humans can make important contributions to the understanding of causal relations between changes in density and a variety of behavioral and physiological changes. It is likely that the application of environmental design to mitigate the noxious effects of density can make some progress in parallel with the experimental studies, but the former area will certainly be materially aided by developments in the latter.

REFERENCES

Barash, David P. (1974) "The Evolution of Marmot Societies: A General Theory." *Science* (2 August):415-20.

Bronson, F. H. and Eleftheriou, B. E. (1964) "Chronic Physiological Effects of Fighting in Mice." *General and Comparative Endocrinology* 4:9-14.

Calhoun, John B. (1962) "Population Density and Social Pathology." *Scientific American* 206:139-48.

_____ (1971) "Control of Population: Numbers," in *Managing the Planet,* edited by Peter Albertson and Margery Barnett. Englewood Cliffs, N.J.: Prentice-Hall. A Spectrum Book.

Christian, John J. (1963) "Endocrine Adaptive Mechanisms and the Physiologic Regulation of Population Growth," in *Physiological Mammalogy,* edited by William V. Mayer and Richard G. Van Gelder. New York: Academic Press.

_____ (1971) "Population Density and Reproductive Efficiency." *Biology of Reproduction* 4:248-94.

_____ and Davis, David E. (1964) "Endocrines, Behavior, and Population." *Science* (18 December):1550-60.

Davis, David E. (1971) "Physiological Effects of Continued Crowding," in Esser, *Behavior and Environment.*

Draper, Patricia (1973) "Crowding Among Hunter-Gatherers: The !Kung Bushmen." *Science* (19 October):301-03.

Esser, Aristide Henri, ed. (1971) *Behavior and Environment: The Use of Space by Animals and Men.* New York-London: Plenum.

Freedman, Jonathan L.; Klevansky, Simon; and Erlich, Paul R. (1971) "The Effect of Crowding on Human Task Performance." *Journal of Applied Social Psychology* 1:7-25.

Freedman; Levy, Alan S.; Buchanan, Roberta Welte; and Price, Judy (1972) "Crowding and Human Aggressiveness." *Journal of Experimental Social Psychology* 8:28-48.

Friedman, S. B. and Ader, R. (1968) "Adrenocortical Response to Novelty and Noxious Stimulation." *Neuroendocrinology* 2:209-12.

Galle, Omer R.; Gove, Walter R.; and McPherson, J. Miller (1972) "Population Density and Pathology: What Are the Relations of Man?" *Science* (7 April):23-30.

Goeckner, Daniel J.; Greenough, William T.; and Mead, William R. (1973) "Deficits in Learning Tasks Following Chronic Overcrowding in Rats." *Journal of Personality and Social Psychology* 28:256-61.

Gregor, Gary L.; Smith, Richard F.; Simons, Lynn S.; and Parker, Howard B. (1972) "Behavioral Consequences of Crowding in the Deermouse (*Peromyscus maniculatus*)." *Journal of Comparative and Physiological Psychology* 79:488-93.

Hall, Edward Twitchell (1966) *The Hidden Dimension*. Garden City, N.Y.: Doubleday.

Krebs, Charles J.; Gaines, Michael S.; Keller, Barry L.; Myers, Judith H.; and Tamarin, Robert H. (1973) "Population Cycles in Small Rodents." *Science* (5 January):35-41.

Leibman, Miriam (1970) "The Effects of Sex and Race Norms on Personal Space." *Environment and Behavior* 2:208-46.

Maier, Steven F.; Seligman, Martin E. P.; and Solomon, Richard L. (1969) "Pavlovian Fear Conditioning and Learned Helplessness: Effects on Escape and Avoidance Behavior of (a) CS-US Contingency and (b) the Independence of the US and Voluntary Responding," in *Punishment and Aversive Behavior*, edited by Byron A. Campbell and Russell M. Church. Century Psychology Series. New York: Appleton-Century-Crofts.

Myers, Kenneth; Hale, C. S.; Mykytowycz, R.; and Hughes, R. L. (1971) "The Effects of Varying Density and Space on Sociality and Health in Animals," in Esser, *Behavior and Environment*.

Olin, Ulla (1966) "Feedback Mechanisms in Human Populations." Paper presented to the Symposium on Population Control at the annual meeting of the American Association for the Advancement of Science, 26-31 December, Washington, D.C.

Ross, Michael; Layton, Bruce; Erickson, Bonnie; and Schopler, John (1973) "Affect, Facial Regard, and Reactions to Crowding." *Journal of Personality and Social Psychology* 28:69-76.

Schorr, Alvin Louis (1963) *Slums and Social Insecurity; An Appraisal of the Effectiveness of Housing Policies in Helping to Eliminate Poverty in the United States*. Washington: U.S. Government Printing Office.

Sommer, Robert (1969) *Personal Space--The Behavioral Basis of Design*. Englewood Cliffs, N.J.: Prentice-Hall.

Southwick, Charles H. (1966) "An Experimental Study of Intragroup Agonistic Behaviour in Rhesus Monkeys (*Macaca mulatta*)." *Behaviour* 28:192-209.

Stokols, Daniel (1972) "On the Distinction Between Density and Crowding: Some Implications for Future Research." *Psychological Review* 79:275-77.

_____ (1973) "The Relation Between Micro and Macro Crowding Phenomena: Some Implications for Environmental Research and Design." *Man-Environment Systems* 3:139-49.

Wynne-Edwards, Vero C. (1965) "Self-Regulating Systems in Populations of Animals." *Science* (26 March):1543-48.

Zlutnick, Steven, and Altman, Irwin (1972) "Crowding and Human Behavior," in *Environment and the Social Sciences: Perspectives and Applications,* edited by Joachim F. Wohlwill and Daniel H. Carson. Washington: American Psychological Association.